THE SPLENDOUR OF
NORWAY
PRAKTFULLE NORGE

CLB 2054
This edition published 1988 by
Knut Aune Kunstforlag A/S Trondheim – Norway
by arrangement with Colour Library Books Ltd, Godalming, Surrey, England.
Text © Colour Library Books Ltd by W. R. Mead.
Captions © Knut Aune Kunstforlag A/S by Bjørn Østraat.
All rights reserved.
Translations: Stewart Clark and Wolfgang Link.
Photographs © Knut Aune Kunstforlag A/S
by Kolbjørn Dekkerhus and Ole P. Rørvik.
ISBN 82-90633-08-4
ART.NR.989

THE SPLENDOUR OF
NORWAY
PRAKTFULLE NORGE

Text by
William Mead

Aune
FORLAG AS
TRONDHEIM · NORWAY

THE SPLENDOUR OF
NORWAY
PRAKTFULLE NORGE

Text by
William Mead

Aune
FORLAG AS
TRONDHEIM · NORWAY

Norge er en sjøfartsnasjon. Lenge før de sjøfarende sagakongene skrev ned sine legender, meislet bronsealderens nybyggere inn de grove omrissene av sine robåter på de ispolerte klippene langs kysten. Deres etterkommere er skipsreder-aristokratiet (som kontrollerer en av verdens største handelsflåter), ingeniørene som konstruerer og vedlikeholder oljeriggene og plattformene i Nordsjøen, de tusener av fiskere som har problemer på grunn av de avtagende fiskeforekomstene i havet, og de titusener av amatørseilere som liver opp sommerbildet med sine seilbåter. Sjøfartstradisjonene understrekes også av de historiske skipene man finner i museene på Bygdøy i Oslo – vikingeskipene, Fridtjof Nansens polarekspedisjonsskip "Fram", Roald Amundsens "Gjøa" og Thor Heyerdahls "Ra" og "Kon-Tiki".

Norge er viet til havet via en uvanlig lang kystlinje. Denne strekker seg over 13 breddegrader. I tillegg kommer Svalbard, det arktiske øyriket ca. 800 kilometer nord for Nordkapp. Av atlaset framgår det at Norges utstrekning er ca. 3000 kilometer fra den brede Oslofjorden i sør til Varangerfjorden ved den russiske grensen i nord. Tatt i betraktning alle buktningere, øyer og holmer i kystlinjen, betyr det at den har en lengde på mere enn 57 000 km.

Norge har bare litt over 4 millioner innbyggere, men reisende som tar hurtigruten langs kysten – uten tvil den mest imponerende sjøreise i Europa – vil alltid ha en eller annen bosetting i sikte. Nordmenn har i uminnelige tider bodd ved sjøen, og det fortsetter de med. De største byene ligger ved sjøen. Oslo, med sin beskjedne Stortingsbygning midt mellom den vakre Akershus festning og det nyklassiske Slottet, har ca. en halv million innbyggere. Bergen, den maleriske, gamle Hansastaden på Vestlandet, ligger omkranset av fjell og hav. Litt lenger sør ligger Stavanger, Norges gullalderby. Her finner man verft for bygging og reparasjon av oljeinstallasjoner vegg i vegg med byens domkirke som er bygd i romansk og gotisk stil. Trondheim, med erkebispesetet og Nidarosdomen hvor Hellig Olavs skrin ble oppbevart, ligger ved den stille Trondheimsfjorden. Byen ligger i det geografiske sentrum av dette langstrakte landet. Den franske forfatter Honoré, de Balzac kalte Norge "Sveits ved havet". De høyeste fjelltoppene, Galdhøpiggen 2469 m og Glittertind 2470 m, (med snøskavl på 18 m) ligger i den romantiske Jotunheimen, "Heimen til Jotnene". Norge er ikke så luftig som Sveits, men man har allikevel en følelse av stor høyde overalt i fjellet. Høydepunktet er likevel fjordene og de bratte fjellsidene på Vestlandet. Hver fjord har sitt særpreg. Lysefjorden med den dramatiske Prekestolen: Nordfjord har respektfulle Loendalen og Oldedalen. Geirangerfjorden med sine anløp av cruiseskip, Sognefjorden og Hardangerfjorden som er de lengste og dypeste, og hvor tidevannet fortsatt er virksomt 120 km fra åpent hav. Fergene som trafikkerer fram og tilbake mellom bygdene passerer under dette panorama av alpetopper og glitrende breer. Her er stupbratte fjellvegger som faller flere hundre meter ned mot fjorden og som går like langt under havflaten. Her er daler som henger over daler, springende fossefall og kaskader av vann. Disse massive inntrykkene får byene til å minne om miniatyrbyer. Sammenlignet med dette blir gårdsbrukene leketøyaktige med sine eventyrlignende uthus og værbitte gårdsbygninger, enger med friskt, grønt gress, frukthager med eple- og kirsebærtrær, velfriserte bringebærbusker og jordbæråkrer. Folk har bosatt seg på de trange hyllene langs kysten og på elvedeltaene alt fra forhistorisk tid. Og overalt har fjellene bakenfor tvunget folk til å vende seg mot havet for å få tilskudd til det daglige brød.

Man opplever et nytt kystklimaks når man kommer til Lofoten nord for Polarsirkelen. Lofotveggen strekker seg over en kystlinje på 120 km. Den består av en kjede værbitte granittklipper omgitt av en lav bølgepolert plattform. På avstand ser den ut som ryggen på en stor drage. Det første avsnittet i Edgar Alan Poes fortelling "En ferd ned i Malstrømmen" begynner her. Tidevannsstrømmen som ble opprinnelsen til denne mytiske malstrømmen, har sitt opphav lenger sør. Den var særskilt avmerket på maritime kart helt fram til tidlig i det 19. århundre.

Det meste av Norges kyst er omgitt av lave, forblåste øyer og skjær, kalt Norges skjærgård. I le av denne finner man leia, en beskyttet skipsled som knytter Norge sammen. På utsiden av skjærene finner man kontinentalsokkelen, undervannsformasjonen som har gitt fiskerne et levebrød i århundrer. Sjøkartene viser navnene på de mange fiskebankene på kontinental sokkelen. I de samme farvannene finner man første generasjon av olje- og naturgassfelt som har fått sine spesielle norske navn – Balder, Odin, Frigg og Heimdal.

På baksiden av denne forblåste, opprevne kysten ligger høye

platåer og vidder. Terrenget her er kupert og steinet, og det er dekket av innsjøer og myrlandskap. Lenger opp i høyden finner man her og der alpine topper. Utover toppene er det spredt et stort antall isbreer, deriblant Jostedalsbreen som er en av de to største i Europa. Nesten to tredjedeler av Norges areal er fjell og vidder.

På landsiden av viddene finner man vertikale daler som ble gravd ut under istiden, og som faller bratt ned i fjordene. Den norske forfatteren Sigurd Hoel har sagt om disse særegne eroderte dalene at de ser ut som om ''de er blitt gravet ut av trollenes ploger''. Avlange fjorder strekker seg langs dalbunnene, og i liene som rager over dem, finner man restene av setrene og sommerbeitene som spilte en betydelig rolle i økonomien i bondesamfunnet i gamle dager. Hver dal – Hallingdal, Gudbrandsdal, Østerdal, Setesdal, Numedal – er like særpreget og selvstendig som hver fjord.

I de mer avskjermete innlandsområdene, spesielt i det østlige av Norge, finner man mye skog. Furu og gran dominerer, og bjørka sprer seg vidt omkring. Langs sydkysten finner man et belte av eik ispedd med noe bøk, og før fjellet tar over har man dvergbjørk og vierkratt. Skogbruksmuseet på Elverum i Østerdalen, som ligger idyllisk til på østsiden av Glomma, gir et godt bilde av økologien og økonomien i skogbruksdistriktene gjennom tidene. På Østlandet finner man også det rikeste jordbrukslandet, spesielt rundt Mjøsa, Norges største innsjø. I innhøstingssesongen er disse distriktene dekket av gule kornåkre. Solide middelalderkirker og noen av Norges største gårdsbruk vitner om velstand og lange tradisjoner i norsk jordbruk. Man finner også produktive jordbruksområder langs Sørlandskysten og ved Trondheimsfjorden. Likevel er mindre enn 4 % av Norges overflate jordbruksland, og ca. 20 % er produktivt skogbruksland.

Selv om Norge ligger så langt nord, har det et bedre klima i forhold til breddegraden enn noe annet land. Grunnen til dette er uløselig knyttet sammen med Golfstrømmen og de vestlige luftstrømmene som dominerer været i Norge. Vegetasjonen gjenspeiler det relativt milde klimaet. Mange trær, busker og planter som hører hjemme i tempererte soner, finnes lenger nord i Norge enn i noe annet land i verden. Blodbøktrærne som vi finner i hager ved Trondheimsfjorden og rhododendronene som trives i Bergens parker og hager, illustrerer dette. Man må heller ikke glemme den marine økologien. Det varme, salte havet, det sterke tidevannet og strømmene holder det isfritt om vinteren og gir liv til en rik flora og fauna. De mange sjødyrartene, utbredelsen til disse og økologien rundt dem, kan man studere i Fiskerimuseet i Bergen. Sjøfugler er også en integrert del av kystøkologien, og disse dekker de enorme fuglefjellene langs den

nordlige del av kysten.

Som et resultat av breddegraden og den opprevne kystlinjen varierer klimaet fra landsdel til landsdel og fra sted til sted. Samtidig er Vest-Norge utsatt for det atlantiske stormsystemet som gir en svært ustabil værtype. Værmeldinger utgjør en tilsvarende viktig del av radioprogrammene. Deler av Vest-Norge har den største nedbørsmengden som er registrert i Europa. Vestlandet er et paraplyland hvor regnet sjelden blir til snø om vinteren. Som kontrast til dette er Østlandet varmere og mer solrikt om sommeren, men har desto kaldere vintre. I le for fjellene i vest, trenger daler som f.eks. Gudbrandsdalen og Ottadalen kunstig vanning for å få en tilfredsstillende avling.

Den nordlige breddegraden gir også en spesiell dagslys- og mørkerytme. Hele Norge opplever lyse sommerkvelder, mens de nordligste fylkene Nordland, Troms og Finnmark har midnattssol om sommeren. I kontrast til dette er det, aller nordligst i landet, mørkt døgnet rundt midtvinters – *Mørketiden*. Man ser Nordlyset oftere i Nord-Norge enn noe annet sted, og dette er gjenstand for vitenskapelige studier ved Nordlys-observatoriet i Tromsø. Nordlys er mer eller mindre bevegelige (blålige) lysninger på klar nattehimmel. Når sola kommer tilbake etter mørketiden, er dette en god anledning til å feire. Barna gleder seg til solfestdagen.

Norge kan glede seg over den dramatiske topografien og det gode klimaet, men ved store snøvintere kan snøskred forekomme i de stupbratte fjellskråningene. Jordskred og oversvømmelser kan også skje ved ekstra store nedbørsmengder. På grunn av at høyfjellet er blitt en nasjonal tumleplass, lærer nordmenn alt fra skoledagene av å respektere fjell og stup. De får opplæring i hvordan de skal omgås disse farene både om vinteren og sommeren, og vernepliktige soldater får i løpet av førstegangstjenesten en grundig og tøff trening i å overleve under vinterforhold. De som bruker innsjøer og havet til adspredelse, bør vise like stor respekt for naturkreftene.

Sommeren er høysesong for fotturister som tar seg fram i fjellet langs nettverket av stier og mellom hyttene som drives av Den Norske Turistforening. Dette er også tiden for fjellklatring (denne sporten har delvis sin opprinnelse i Norge) og bruk av fritidsbåter (båtbyggerkunsten praktiseres fortsatt mange steder). Om vinteren dominerer skisport friluftsbildet. Fram til forrige århundre var ski hyppigere benyttet som framkomstmiddel om vinteren enn vanlige kjøretøyer. Norge er skisportens hjemland, noe som understrekes av alle skiuttrykkene i språket. Skimuseet i Oslo viser skisportens historie på en enkel, men virkningsfull måte. Dette har vært en mannsdominert sport, men fra forrige århundre fikk sporten også kvinnelige utøvere.

Det er i løpet av siste generasjon at Norge er blitt effektivt knyttet sammen av et landbasert kommunikasjonsnett. Moderne ingeniørkunst og utstyr har vært helt nødvendig for bygging og vedlikehold av veier og flyplasser, og ikke minst for bygging av nødvendige tunneler i vanskelig terreng. Norge har flere tunnelmeter pr. innbygger enn noe annet land. Den lengste veitunnelen er på strekningen Gudevangen – Flåm i Sognefjorden er 11,2 km. lang. (Åpner i 1991). Veinettet er i dag meget godt utbygget, og på E6 er det kun ett sted man må ta ferge. (Over Tysfjord i Nordland). Det er ellers en mengde ferger som går over fjorder og mellom øyer langs Norges lange kyst. Luftfarten har forenklet persontransporten svært mye, og den har stimulert økonomien og lettet tilgjengeligheten av velferdsgoder. Spesialiserte helsetilbud kan konsentreres mer effektivt og helikopterambulanser kan ta seg av nødutrykkinger til isolerte steder. Helikoptre har også vært en velsignelse for bygging og vedlikehold av kraft- og telefonlinjer i ulendt terreng.

Integreringen man ser i Norge i dag er et nytt fenomen. I 1906, da unionen med Sverige opphørte og Norge ble en selvstendig nasjon, var innbyggerne løsere knyttet sammen enn de er i dag. Hver dal og fjord utgjorde sitt eget samfunn. Forskjellige dialekter, vaner, tradisjoner, byggeskikker, ingeniørkunst og overtro ble bevart på grunn av den isolerte beliggenheten. Disse særpregene kan man studere i lokale og regionale folkemuseer. F. eks. kan man på "Folkemuseet på Bygdøy" eller i "De Sandvigske Samlinger" på Lillehammer se enestående eksempler på dette. Paradoksalt nok fant denne utviklingen sted samtidig som Norge utviklet seg sakte og var relativt fattig i det industrialiserende Vest-Europa, og samtidig som en strøm av emigranter reiste til den nye verden. Denne tiden var også en blomstringstid for patriotiske diktere som gav et romantisk skjær til de nasjonale følelsene og fyrte oppunder og kultiverte fram et landsmål som skulle utfordre riksmålet som hadde sine røtter i Norges Danmarksperiode. Til samme tidsperiode hørte også noen få framsynte antikvarer som tok vare på restene av de spesielle stavkirkene før modernistene byttet dem ut med uniforme hvitspirete plankebygninger.

I mellomtiden skrev Henrik Ibsen sin berømmelige Peer Gynt. Misdannete og hårete troll (kvinneutgaven av denne arten sparket og hadde hale) og draugen (vanntrollet) fikk et visuelt uttrykk, og en hel skole av romantiske kunstnere gjenskapte disse idylliske landskapene og koselige bondeinteriørene. Dette var tidsperioden før industrialistene oppfostret realister som f. eks. Edvard Munch, med sine mesterstykker av nevrotiske byscener, og Gustav Vigeland som med sin monumentale representasjon av menneskeheten dominerer Frognerparken i Oslo med sine skulpturer.

Jordbruk, skogbruk, fiske og gruvedrift som var hovednærings-

veiene i dette samfunnet, skulle nå bli forandret til et service- og produksjonssamfunn. De små gårdsbrukene ble eid av de som bodde der (Norge hadde ikke noe føydalsystem), og de drev mest med husdyr. Man kan fortsatt høre sau- og kubjeller i utmarkene, og flokker med geiter kan til og med ta tilflukt i veitunneler. Jordbruket er sterkt subsidiert, og det må være det i det arktiske Norge hvor vekstsesongen er så kort som fem måneder enkelte steder. Noen ganger ser man skogbruk kombinert med jordbruk. Dette er spesielt tilfelle på Østlandet hvor tømmeret utgjør råmaterialet for den store papir- og celluloseindustrien langs Oslofjorden. Noen ganger kombineres fiske og jordbruk. Yrkesfiskere med sine kooperativt eide trålere og sitt kostbare utstyr står for store deler av fangsten. Likevel deltar fortsatt mindre bruk i vintertorskefisket i Lofoten og vårsildefisket i Møre og Romsdal. I lange tider har selfangst vært en tilleggsnæring, mens den eldgamle hvalindustrien (som i realiteten brakte norske interesser til Antarktis) er lagt ned. I kontrast til dette står den økende aktiviteten av oppdrettsfisk, som stadig utgjør en økende andel i fiskerinæringen. Det finnes så mange som 700 oppdrettsanlegg for laks langs kysten. Mink- og revefarming er også svært lønnsomt. Tamreindrift, fortrinnsvis i Troms og Finnmark, forblir et yrke for spesialister. Det årevisse trekket av tamrein utgjør ca. 200 000 dyr. Idag er samene beskjeftiget som bønder, fiskere og reinsdyrgjetere, hvor sistnevnte kategori er i mindretall.

Metallbearbeiding er blitt utført av spesialiserte håndverkere helt siden siste del av jernaldertidens smeder produserte brynjer for vikingene ved hjelp av trekull og myrmalm. I de kongelige sølvgruvene på Kongsberg har nå turistenes ekko avløst generasjoner av gruvearbeidere som arbeidet i gruvegangene. Koppergruvene på den kalde Rørosvidda og i det arktiske Kåfjord har lenge vært nedlagt, selv om det fortsatt utvinnes svovelkis. Kobolten fra Haugfoss mistet verdensmonopolet da I.G.Farben presenterte sitt kjemiske farge-substitutt. Men fortsatt drives små årer som inneholder kostbare metaller som f. eks. molybden og titan, mens store dagbrudd avdekker magre jernmalmårer på sørsiden av Varangerfjorden.

Det er et annerledes mineral som beriker Norge i dag. Blant alle nasjoner i Vest-Europa har det falt i Norges lodd å være beriket med olje og naturgass. Geologene har bekreftet at det finnes enorme forekomster på feltene i Nordsjøen, langs vestkysten og i Barentshavet. Etter hvert som de tekniske problemene med utvinning i disse tøffe farvannene er redusert, har man fortsatt ikke kommet fram til en politisk avtale om den maritime grensen mot Sovjet i Arktis. I mellomtiden utvinner både Norge og Sovjet kull på Svalbard, hvor et samfunn på 1500 nordmenn produserer ca. 500 000 tonn pr. år.

Bare en beskjeden andel av Norges energiressurser kommer fra termiske kilder. Topografi og klima i kombinasjon med overveldende ressurser av vannkraft, avansert utstyr og effektiv langdistanseoverføring av elektrisk kraft, gjør at hydroelektrisk kraft er blitt en sentral del av dagliglivet i Norge. Dikteren Bjørnstjerne Bjørnson levde lenge nok til å være vitne til (med hans egne ord) "tumlende fossefall forvandlet til lys". Utnyttelsesgraden har økt etter hvert som man har fått bedre utstyr og etter hvert som de største vassdragene er blitt utnyttet bedre. Store sjøer er ført sammen og ledet fram til de store fallene hvor man kan oppnå maksimal effekt. Mye potensiale ligger tilbake, men utnyttelsen av vannkraft er gjenstand for økende motstand. Både bevaringstilhengere og de som lever av turisme utfordrer utbyggerne. Kontroversene om Vøringfossen, som stupte over kanten av Hardangervidda og ned i den dype Måbødalen, illustrerer dette.

Mens utviklingen av vannkraft ennå var en ung teknikk, var hydroelektrisk kraft relativt rimelig, og kraftkrevende industri som f. eks. aluminiumsverk hadde store økonomiske fordeler. I dag er behovet for elektrisk kraft blitt så stort at man kan oppleve regionale og sesongmessige leveringsproblemer. Det virker som om maksimalbelastningen inntreffer om vinteren og faller sammen med de reduserte vannmengdene man har på denne årstiden. Det økende behovet for elektrisk kraft gjenspeiler både den endrede oppbyggingen av industrien og den høyere levestandarden. De elektrometallurgiske og elektrokjemiske konsernene er de største forbrukerne. Blant disse finner vi kjemigiganten Norsk Hydro, som holder til på Herøya ved Porsgrunn. Det statlig eide Jernverket i Mo i Rana i Nordland ble utviklet med tanke på å gi aktivitet i et område med stor arbeidsløshet og dårlig utviklet næringsliv. Jernverket forsynes med elektrisk kraft fra et stort kraftverk i Røssåga. Et følsomt element i den norske økonomien er samfunn med bare en industribedrift. Det finnes over 70 slike ensidige industrisamfunn i Norge, og de er alle svært følsomme overfor markedssvingningene. Som et resultat av dette har noen bedrifter stagnert, og noen har trappet ned aktiviteten. Dette gir i sin tur sosiale problemer i lokalsamfunnet. Man ser at samfunnet og økonomien langt oftere hadde kommet opp i konfliktsituasjoner med hverandre hvis det ikke hadde vært for oljeutvinningen og de mulighetene denne gir til å betale stadig større subsidier. Dette fører til ytterligere problemer da 50% av Norges eksport kommer fra oljen som er avhengig av et følsomt verdensmarked.

Men disse betraktningene faller ikke akkurat den besøkende i øyet.

Den besøkende vil istedet underkaste seg trolldommen ved Norge. De dramatiske kontrastene det norske samfunnet byr på er en effektfull turistattraksjon. På den ene siden har man de ville og forblåste landskapene med stedsnavn som synes å være hugget ut av stein – Klett, Kvam, Kvål, Sjåk. På den andre siden finner man rolige områder som minner om Edens Have om sommeren (eller "Nisseland" om vinteren). Paradis er faktisk navnet på en bydel i Bergen. Dette understrekes også av stedsnavnet Hell (en liten grend i Trøndelag). Man vil fort oppdage at Norge er et land som er bedre å leve i for unge og eldre enn de fleste andre land. For barn er det et eventyrrike, spesielt fordi de fleste familiene enten eier eller har adgang til en hytte ved sjøen eller på fjellet. For de eldre er det godt å vite at bare folk i Sverige og på Island har høyere levealder. Besøkende fra overbefolkede land oppdager med tilfredsstillelse et land "with more space where nobody is than where anybody is", (sitat fra Gertrude Stein).

De store ubebodde områdene og sjøen har uten tvil fostret fram selvsikkerhet og uavhengighet. Evnen til å stå på egne ben som den perfekte etterkommer av Ibsen. Slike kvaliteter finner man det beste uttrykk for i Hjemmefrontbevegelsen under 2. verdenskrig. Dette førte også til det overveldende flertallet mot medlemskap i E.F. Disse holdningene kan heller ikke skilles fra det faktum at de fleste nordmenn fortsatt har sine røtter på, eller lever i nær kontakt med landsbygda. Dette forklarer også at de fleste nordmenn setter pris på det enkle og har evnen til å uttrykke sin glede over dagligdagse ting til andre. En besøkende får uten tvil mest ut av sitt Norgesopphold hvis han eller hun kan ta del i den sorgløse munterheten som tradisjonene, folkesangen og folkedansen gir. Man får også større utbytte av besøket hvis man er interessert i håndverk, hvis man setter pris på en Griegmelodi, og hvis man kan bli opphisset av den patriotiske feiringen av 17. mai med sine barnetog, taler og flagg. Sjelden kan et steds atmosfære være slik i harmoni med menneskene som i Norge. Det er ganske enkelt et stort hell at dette tiltalende landet har en nasjonalsang som må være en av verdens mest melodiøse, og hvor man gleder seg med ord som ikke er vanskelige å synge: Ja, vi elsker dette landet.

Norway is a kingdom of the sea. Long before the sea kings of the sagas recorded their legends, Bronze Age settlers chiselled the crude outlines of their rowboats on the ice-polished rocks along the shoreline. Their logical descendants are the aristocracy of shipowners (who control one of the world's largest merchant navies), the engineers who have built and who maintain the oil rigs and platforms in Norway's offshore waters, the thousands of fishermen who are troubled by the diminishing harvest of the sea, and the tens of thousands of amateur sailors whose leisure boats enliven the summer scene. The kingdom of the sea is also proclaimed by the historical ships that draw the nautically-minded to the museums at Bygdø, Oslo, which exhibit Viking ships, Fridtjof Nansen's Fram, which he used on his polar expeditions, Roald Amundsen's Gjøa, and Thor Heyerdahl's Ra and Kon-Tiki.

Norway is married to the sea through an exceptionally long seaboard. It extends through thirteen degrees of latitude, excluding Svalbard and the Arctic archipelago some 800 kilometres beyond North Cape. Though the outline of Norway is some 3,000 km. in length from the broad Oslofjord in the south to Varangerfjord on the Russian border, when all the islands and skerries are taken into account, together with the indentations in the coastline, the total length is over 57,000 km.

There are only just over four million inhabitants in Norway, but travellers who take the steamer along the magnificent coast – undoubtedly the most impressive voyage anywhere in Europe – are never out of sight of some form of settlement. The majority of Norwegians have always lived beside the sea and continue to do so. The principal cities are on the coast. Oslo, with its modest parliament building midway between the fine Akershus fortress and the neo-classical royal palace, has some half million inhabitants. Bergen, the picturesque old Hanseatic settlement on the west coast, lies surrounded by mountains and sea. Further south is Stavanger, Norway's boom town, where yards for building and repairing oil installations stand cheek-by-jowl with its romanesque cathedral. Trondheim lies by the quiet waters of Trondheimfjord, at what might be called the geographical fulcrum of this lengthy land, and contains Nidaros Cathedral, the shrine of Norway's patron saint, Olaf.

The French author Honoré de Balzac called Norway 'Switzerland by the sea'! The highest peaks, Galdhøpiggen (2,469 metres), and Glittertind, (2,470 metres) – capped by an 18 metre snowdrift – are in the romantically-named Jotunheim, 'the Home of the Giants'. Thus, whilst Norway is by no means as lofty as Switzerland, there is, nevertheless, a feeling of great height everywhere in the mountains. A climax is reached in the fjords and fells of the western seaboard. Each fjord has its distinctive features. Lysefjord has dramatic pulpit

rock; Nordfjord has the awesome Loen valley; Geirangerfjord claims the record for visiting cruise ships, and Sognefjord and Hardangerfjord, where the tide still pulses 120 km. from the open sea, are the longest and deepest. The ferries that ply a year-round shuttle between the settlements pass beneath a panorama of alpine peaks and glistening glaciers; an area of sheer rock walls that fall vertically several hundred metres into the fjords and continue just as far underwater. Here are valleys hanging above other valleys, leaping cataracts and veils of water. Such massive features dwarf the towns and villages. They give a toy-town appearance to the otherwise sturdy farmsteads, with their fortress-like outhouses and colour-washed dwellings, their aprons of bright green grass, orchards of apple and cherry trees, and trim rows of raspberries and strawberries. Their sites, on the narrow coastal terraces and river deltas, have been occupied since prehistoric times. And always, the mountains behind have forced them to look to the sea to supplement a meagre living.

A second coastal climax is encountered in the Lofoten Islands north of the Arctic Circle. Lofotveggen, the Lofoten wall, extends for some 120 km. seaward. It consists of a chain of weathered granite peaks surrounded by a low, wave-washed platform. From a distance it looks like a great dragon's back. Edgar Alan Poe's story The Descent into the Maelstrøm begins here. The tidal rush of waters that gave rise to the mythical maelstrøm occurs farther south. It continued to be marked as a feature on maritime charts until the early nineteenth century.

Much of Norway's coast is girdled by low, rugged islands and skerries called the skærgard by Norwegians. The channels to the leeward side constitute a protected shipping lane which ties Norway together. Seawards from the skerries is the continental shelf, the submarine topography of which has been of concern to fishermen through the centuries. Sea charts bear the names of its many fishing banks. In these same waters are the first generation of oil and natural gas fields, with their distinctly Norwegian names: Balder, Odin, Frigg, Heimdal.

Back from the barren, dissected coast lie extensive high plateaus, or vidder. They are undulating and rocky, and are covered with lakes and bogs. Rising above them are occasional clusters of alpine peaks; and a number of glaciers, including Jostedalsbre, one of the largest in Europe. Nearly two-thirds of this surface of Norway consists of mountains and plateaus.

On the landward side of the vidder, there are the vertically-sided valleys, deepened during the Ice Age, falling steeply into the fjords. In the words of the Norwegian novelist Sigurd Hoel, these distinctively eroded dales, look 'as though they have been dug out by troll's ploughs'. Ribbon lakes are strung along the valley floors, while on the high shoulders of land that jut over them are the remains of the summer pastures or seters that were once such a typical feature of the rural economy. Each dale – Hallingdal, Gudbrandsdal, Østerdal, Setesdal, Numedal – is as distinctive and self-contained as each fjord.

The more sheltered inland areas, especially those of eastern Norway, are heavily wooded. Pine and spruce dominate, birches are widely scattered, there is a belt of oaks and some beech along the south coast and a zone of dwarf birches and willows at higher altitudes before reaching the mountains. The forestry museum at Elverum in Østerdal, idyllically situated on the east of the Glommen River, provides an excellent picture of the ecology and economy of these forested areas through the ages. The east also has the richest farmlands, in particular around Mjøsen, Norway's largest lake. At harvest time it is flanked with yellow grainfields. Sturdy mediaeval churches and some of Norway's largest farms are a testimony to the long-established wealth of its agriculture. There are also productive farmlands along the south coast and around Trondheimfjord. Nevertheless, less than four per cent of the surface area of Norway is cultivated and about twenty per cent is productive forest.

Although Norway lies so far north, it enjoys a more favoured climate in relation to its latitude than any other country. This is because of the Gulf Stream and the westerly airflow that dominates Norwegian weather. Vegetation reflects the relative mildness of the climate, and many temperate zone trees, shrubs and plants have a more northerly occurrence in Norway than anywhere else in the world. The copper beech trees in gardens around Trondheimsfjord, and the rhodedendrons that thrive in Bergen's parks and gardens illustrate the point. Nor must marine ecology be forgotten. The relatively warm sea-water, strong in tides and currents and free from ice in winter, supports a rich flora and fauna. The diversity of sea creatures, their habitats, and the nature of the economy built upon them are brought to life in the Fishery museum in Bergen. Seabirds are also an integral part of the coastal ecology, clouding the stupendous bird cliffs along northern parts of the coast.

As a result of its latitudinal range and highly dissected relief, Norway's climate varies greatly from region to region. At the same time, western Norway's exposure to the Atlantic cyclonic systems produces a very unstable weather pattern. Weather bulletins occupy a correspondingly long time on radio programmes. Parts of western Norway have the highest precipitation recorded anywhere in Europe. It is umbrella country, where it rains rather than snows in the winter. Contrastingly, eastern Norway enjoys warmer and brighter summers, though colder winters. In the lee of the mountains

to the west are valleys such as Gudbrandsdal and Ottadal, which require sprinkler irrigation for satisfactory cropping.

The high latitude also results in a marked seasonal rhythm of daylight and darkness. The whole of Norway experiences light summer nights, while the northern counties of Troms, Finnmark and Nordland enjoy the midnight sun in summer. In contrast to this, in the very far north there is the midwinter darkness – Mørketiden. The Aurora borealis, occurs in north Norway with greater frequency than anywhere else and is the subject of scientific research at an institute in Tromsø. The Aurora borealis is a swaying, bluish light phenomenon which is seen when the night sky is clear. The return of the sun after midwinter gloom is an occasion for festivities, and children in the north look forward to parties on the day the sun returns.

Though Norway gains considerable advantages from its dramatic topology and favourable climate, there is a price to pay in winters with a lot of snow, when there is a risk of thundering avalanches roaring down the precipitous mountain sides. If rainfall is excessive, this may lead to mudslides and floods. As the vast mountain areas have become national recreation centres, Norwegians are taught from their schooldays onwards to respect the mountains and rock faces. They receive both winter and summer instruction in coping with hazards, while conscripts doing their military service are subject to arduous training in winter conditions. A different, but no less strict, discipline is demanded of those who take to the seas and lakes for recreation.

Summer is the great season for trekking over the network of highland paths between the mountain lodges run by the century-old Tourist Association. It is also the time for mountaineering (the sport was partly pioneered in Norway) and for yachting (with the art of boat-building still being meticulously practised). Winter is the season for skiing. Until the present century, the ski was of more use than the wheel for winter communication. Norway was the birthplace of skiing – as the vocabulary of the sport clearly indicates. The ski museum in Oslo presents the history of the sport in a simple but effective manner. Though this sport has very clearly been one that is male-dominated, from the last century onwards women have been brought more and more into the picture.

It is only over the last generation that Norway has been efficiently knitted together by a system of overland communications. Modern engineering techniques and equipment have been critical in highway and airfield construction and maintenance, especially for tunnelling to ease the passage through the difficult terrain. Norway may have more road tunnels per capita than any other country – the longest road tunnel, between Gudvangen and Flå in Sognefjord, some 11. km., opens in 1991. Today's road network is something the country can be proud of, and on the main E6 highway there is only one ferry crossing remaining (across the Tysfjord in Nordland). Numerous ferries criss-cross the fjords and connect the islands and the mainland all along the extensive coast of Norway. Air transport has simplified life for everyone in the country, apart from stimulating the economy and easing the provision of welfare services. Specialised hospital facilities are more efficiently concentrated as helicopter ambulances can deal with emergencies in isolated settlements. In difficult country, the helicopter has also been a boon for construction and maintenance of the power cables and telephone lines.

The present-day integration of Norway is a new phenomenon. In 1906, when the old nation severed its connection with the Swedish Crown and became a young sovereign state, the population was loosely strung together. Each dale and fjord retained a community life of its own. Distinctive dialects, customs, folk lore, building styles, designs and superstitions were preserved in isolation. Some measure of their diversity is to be seen in the local and regional folk museums. The Folk Museum at Bygdøy, Oslo and the one in eastern Norway are outstanding examples. Paradoxically, they had their origin at the same time that Norway was sensing its backwardness and relative poverty during the industrialisation of western Europe and a stream of emigrants was leaving for the New World. The time was also the heyday of the patriotic poets, who cast a romantic glow over national feeling and seized upon and cultivated a country language (landsmål) to challenge the official language (riksmål) which had its roots in Norway's Danish period. A few far-sighted antiquarians belonged to the same period and preserved the remains of remarkable mediaeval stave churches before the modernists replaced them with uniformly white-spired and clapboard buildings.

Meanwhile, Henrik Ibsen conceived his adventurous Peer Gynt. Deformed, hairy trolls (the female of the species was hoofed and tailed) and the draug (or water sprite) were all given visual form, and a school of romantic artists projected idyllic landscapes and snug peasant interiors. These were the days before industrialists motivated latter-day realists such as Edward Munch, with his masterpieces of the neurotic urban scene, and Gustav Wigeland, whose monumental representations of mankind sculpted in stone dominate Oslo's Frogner Park.

The farming, forestry, fishing and mining that provided the principal means of livelihood in this setting have now been subordinated to service industries and manufacturing. The small, owner-occupied farms – for Norway knew no feudal system – are mostly concerned with animal husbandry. Sheep and cattle bells still ring in the grazing areas and herds of goats may even take shelter in road tunnels. Farming is heavily subsidised – and needs to be in Arctic Norway, where the growing period is as little as five months. Sometimes forestry is combined with farming. This is especially so in eastern Norway, the timber stands providing the raw materials for the large paper and pulp plants around Oslofjord. Sometimes fishing and farming are combined. Professional fishermen, with their cooperatively-owned trawlers and expensive gear, account for increasing quantities of the catch, but smaller operators still join in the spring cod fisheries off Lofoten and the spring herring fisheries off Møre and Romsdal in the west. For a long time, sealing was a subsidiary pursuit, while the age-old whaling industry (which eventually carried Norwegian interests to Antarctica) has been allowed to run down. Contrastingly, fish farming increasingly supplements rural incomes. There are, for example, no less than 700 salmon farms. Mink and fox farming are equally profitable. Reindeer husbandry, principally in the counties of Troms and Finnmark, remains a specialist operation. The seasonally-migrant domestic herds total some 200,000. Today, the ethnically-distinct Lapps (or, more correctly, Samer) are occupationally classified as farmers, fishermen and reindeer herders, the last category being the smallest.

Metal-working has commanded the attention of specialist craftsmen from the end of the Iron Age, when smiths produced accoutrements for the Vikings from local bog ore and charcoal. The royal silver mines at Kongsberg now echo to the feet of tourists instead of the generations of miners who worked the deposits. Copper ores from the bleak Røros vidda and from the Arctic Kåfjord have long since been spent, though pyrites are still mined. The cobalt of Haugfoss lost a world monopoly when I.G. Farben introduced substitute chemical dyes. But pockets of critical ores such as molybdenum and titanium are mined, while huge open-cast workings yield lean iron ores on the south side of Varangerfjord.

It is a different kind of mineral that enriches Norway today. Among western European nations, Norway has become the heir to a lion's share of oil and natural gas. And geologists have confirmed that there are generous reserves beyond the North Sea fields, off the northwest coast and in the Barents Sea. While the technical difficulties of extraction in these hazardous waters have been reduced, the political problem of agreeing upon the Arctic maritime boundary with the U.S.S.R. awaits solution. Meanwhile, coal continues to be mined by both Norway and the U.S.S.R. on the Svalbard archipelago, where a community of 1,500 Norwegians produces some 500,000 tons a year.

But only a modest amount of Norway's energy derives from thermal sources, for topography and climate in combination endow it with abundant hydroelectricity. Given large-scale equipment and effective long- distance transmission, hydroelectric power became a central feature of Norwegian life. The poet Bjørnstjerne Bjørnson lived long enough to witness (in his words) the 'tumbling torrents...turned to light'. Increasingly elaborate schemes have been conceived as the principal sites have been harnessed. High level lake systems have been strung together and conduited to the plateau edges, where the maximum head of water can be achieved. Much potential remains, but the harnessing of waterfalls is subject to increasing constraints. Both conservationists and those who promote the tourist trade challenge the developers. The controversy over Voringfoss, plunging over the edge of Hardangervidda into the deep trough of Måbodal illustrates this point.

In the earlier days of its development, hydroelectric power was relatively cheap and branches of industry such as aluminium processing benefitted considerably. Today, the demand for energy is so great that there may be regional and seasonal supply problems. Thus, peak demand tends to occur in winter, which coincides with a reduction in the flow of water. The increased demand for energy reflects both the changing nature of industry and higher living standards. The electro-metallurgical and electro-chemical industries are the major consumers. Among them is the chemical giant Norsk Hydro, with its huge plant on Herøya near Porsgrunn. The state-owned iron and steel plant at Moi Rana in Nordland, created in order to foster activity in an area of unemployment and under-development, is linked to a major power scheme at Røssåga. A sensitive feature of the Norwegian economy is the single-industry community. There are over seventy of these in Norway and all are vulnerable to market conditions. As a result, some stagnate and some decline, which gives rise to severe local social difficulties. Despite this, society and the economy would come into conflict more frequently but for the fact that oil revenues are available to pay for often generous subsidisation. However, this leads to a further problem, because the fifty per cent of Norway's exports accounted for by oil are subject to a volatile world market. But these are considerations that do not impinge directly upon the visitor.

The visitor, indeed, will submit readily to the spell of Norway. The dramatic contrasts in the scenic backdrop to life are a powerful tourist attraction. On the one hand there are the wild and barren landscapes, many of whose names seem to be carved out of stone – Klett, Kvam, Kvål, Skjåk. On the other hand there are tamed and civilised terrains that suggest Gardens of Eden in summer (or a Father Christmas land in winter). Paradise, in fact, is the name of a settlement which is now part of Bergen's suburbs. It appropriately complements Hell (a hamlet in Trøndelag county). It will rapidly become evident to the visitor that Norway is a country which accommodates both young and old more easily than most others. For children, it is an adventure land, especially as most families either own or have access to a cottage by the sea or in the mountains. For the elderly, it is good to know that only Sweden and Iceland can claim equal life expectancy. For visitors from crowded countries, it is a joy (to use the phrase of Gertrude Stein) to encounter a land 'with more space where nobody is than where anybody is'.

Doubtless the open spaces of land and sea have fostered the attitude of self reliance and independence – the ability to stand alone – that characterises the perfect Ibsenite. Such qualities found their ultimate expression in the wartime resistance movement. Equally, they may have led a popular vote to reject membership of the E.E.C. Nor can such attitudes be divorced from the fact that most Norwegians have their roots in, and retain their connection with, the countryside. In turn, this background may help to explain the capacity of most of them to relish the simple things of life and to communicate that enjoyment to others. Certainly the visitors who will get the most out of Norway are those who can share in the innocent merriment of folk lore, folk song and folk dancing; who can enjoy rural craftsmanship; who can appreciate an evocative Grieg melody, and who can still be stirred by the patriotic bravura of May 17 (Constitution Day), with its processions, pageants, speeches and flag-waving. Rarely does the genius loci and the spirit of a people appear to be in such harmony as in Norway. And is it simply good fortune that this appealing land should have acquired a national anthem which must be among the world's most tuneful, and which rejoices in words that are not an embarrassment to sing? Ja vi elsker dette landet – Yes, we love this country.

Norwegen ist ein Reich der See. Lange bevor die sagenumwobenen Könige der Meere ihre Geschichten niederschrieben, meißelten Siedler des Bronzezeitalters die groben Umrisse ihrer Ruderboote in die vom Eis polierten Felsen entlang der Küste. Zu ihrer Nachkommenschaft gehören: die Aristokratie der Schiffseigner (der eine der Welt größten Handelsmarinen untersteht); die Ingenieure, die vor der Küste Norwegens Bohrinseln gebaut haben und sie jetzt instandhalten; die Tausende von Fischern, die sich mit immer kleineren Fängen zufrieden geben müssen, und schließlich die Zehntausende von Hobby-Seglern, deren Freizeit-Boote im Sommer die Szene beleben. Den Beinamen "Reich der See" hat Norwegen auch wegen der historischen Schiffe verdient, die ein seefahrtsbegeistertes Publikum in die Museen von Bygdøy in Oslo locken. Dort sind alte Wikinger-Schiffe ausgestellt, aber auch Fridtjof Nansens "Fram" (das Boot, mit dem er seine Polarexpeditionen unternommen hat), oder auch Roald Amundsens "Gjøa" sowie Thor Heyerdahls "Ra" und "Kon Tiki".

Norwegens Bündnis mit der See ist durch eine ungewöhnlich lange Küste besiegelt. Die Küstenlinie erstreckt sich über dreizehn geographische Breitengrade. Svalbard und das arktische Archipel (800 km nördlich des Nordkaps) sind dabei nicht mitgezählt. Der Umfang Norwegens beträgt 3000 km, gemessen vom breiten Oslofjord im Süden bis zum Varangerfjord an der russischen Grenze. Würde man alle Inseln und Schären berücksichtigen und auch die Einkerbungen der Küste mitmessen, käme man auf einen Umfang von 57000 km.

Norwegen hat nur etwas über vier Millionen Einwohner. Aber Reisende, die mit dem Dampfer die faszinierende Küste entlangfahren – was zweifellos eine der beeindruckendsten Schiffsreisen in ganz Europa ist –, werden fast überall auf Lebenszeichen stoßen. Schon immer hat der Großteil der norwegischen Bevölkerung in Küstennähe gelebt, und daran wird sich wohl auch nichts ändern. Alle bedeutenden Städte des Landes liegen an der Küste. Die Landeshauptstadt Oslo hat eine halbe Million Einwohner und ist bekannt für ihr bescheidenes Parlamentsgebäude, das in der Mitte zwischen der eindrucksvollen Festung Akershus und dem neo-klassizistischen Königspalast liegt. Die malerische alte Hansestadt Bergen ist an der Westküste gelegen und von Gebirgszügen und Meer umgeben. Weiter südlich ist Stavanger, eine Stadt, deren Gesicht deutlich vom Öl-Boom geprägt worden ist. Hier findet man im Schatten der romanischen Kathedrale Hinterhöfe und Werksgelände, auf denen Ölbohranlagen montiert und repariert werden. Trondheim spiegelt sich im ruhigen Wasser des Trondheimfjords und könnte als geographischer Mittelpunkt des Landes gelten. Hier steht die Nidaros-Kathedrale, Grabstätte für Norwegens Schutzheiligen Olaf.

Der französische Schriftsteller Honoré de Balzac hat Norwegen einmal "Schweiz am Meer" genannt. Von den beiden höchsten Gipfeln Galdhøppigen und Glittertind – 2469 und 2470 Meter hoch und bedeckt mit einer 18 Meter tiefen Schneedeckann man herabschauen auf eine Gebirgslandschaft mit dem romantischen Namen Jötunheimen, was soviel heißt wie "Heim der Riesen". Obwohl Norwegen längst nicht so hohe Gipfel aufweist wie die Schweiz, erscheinen einem die Berge sehr hoch. Bei den Fjorden und Fjells an der Westküste sind die Bergspitzen am höchsten.

Kein Fjord ist wie der andere. Der Lysefjord zum Beispiel ist für seine beeindruckenden Felssäulen bekannt, beim Nordfjord findet man das ehrfurchtsgebietende Loen-Tal, der Geirangerfjord hält den Rekord über Besuche von Passagierschiffen, und der Sognefjord sowie der Hardangerfjord sorgen dafür, daß man auch 120 km von der Küste entfernt im Landesinnern noch Ebbe und Flut spürt. Damit sind diese beiden Fjorde die längsten und tiefsten. Über die Fähren, die das ganze Jahr über zwischen den Siedlungen pendeln, dominiert ein Panorama aus Gebirgsgipfeln und glitzernden Gletschern. Die Fähren passieren Gebiete, wo kahle Felswände – hunderte von Metern hoch – senkrecht ins Wasser abfallen und selbst unter der Wasseroberfläche erst nach mehreren hundert Metern enden. Hier gibt es Täler, die über anderen Tälern hängen, reißende Stromschnellen und rauschende Wasserfälle. Derart beeindruckende Naturwunder lassen die Städte und Dörfer winzig erscheinen. Wie Spielzeughäuser wirken plötzlich die großen Gehöfte mit burgähnlichen Seitenhäusern und farbgetünchten Wohnhäusern, mit riesigen, saftiggrünen Wiesen und Obstgärten, in denen Apfelbäume, Kirschbäume, lange Reihen von Himbeersträuchern und Erdbeerstauden wachsen. Der Grund und Boden, auf dem diese Anwesen stehen – auf den Küstenterrassen oder in einem Flußdelta – wurden schon in prähistorischer Zeit bewohnt. Und immer – mit den Bergen im Rücken – mußte mit dem, was das Meer bot, das karge Leben aufgebessert werden.

Auf einen weiteren landschaftlichen Höhepunkt in Küstennähe stößt man bei den Lofoten, oberhalb des nördlichen Polarkreises: Lofotveggen, der Lofoten-Wall, erstreckt sich 120 km lang seewärts. Er besteht aus einer Kette von verwitterten Granitbrocken, die von einer wellenumspülten Plattform umgeben ist. Aus der Ferne ähnelt dieser Wall dem Rücken eines Drachen. Edgar Alan Poes Geschichte "Der Untergang im Malstrom" beginnt hier. Die geheimnisvollen Strömungen des mythischen Malstrom findet man weiter südlich. Bis ins frühe 19. Jahrhundert hinein waren diese Strömungen in den Meereskarten verzeichnet.

An vielen Stellen ist die Küste Norwegens gesäumt von niedrigen, zerklüfteten Inseln und Schären, von den Norwegern "Skaergard" genannt. Die Meerengen zwischen Inseln und Festland stellen eine geschützte Fahrrinne für Schiffe dar, die gleichzeitig Norwegen zusammenhält. Zum Meer hinaus sind den Schären Riffe vorgelagert, deren Lagebeschreibung für die Fischer seit Jahrhunderten von großer Bedeutung sind. Auf den Seekarten liest man auch die Namen der dortigen Fischgründe. In denselben Gewässern findet man aber auch die erste Generation der Gas- und Ölfelder mit ihren typisch norwegischen Namen: Balder, Odin, Frigg, Heimdal.

Hinter der kargen, zerstückelten Küste breiten sich weite Plateaus aus, "Fjell" genannt. Sie sind hügelig, felsig, und von Seen und Sümpfen bedeckt. An einigen Stellen wird die Landschaft von Gipfelgruppen überragt; auch einige Gletscher gibt es, darunter Jostedalsbre, der zu den größten Gletschern Europas gehört. Fast zwei Drittel der norwegischen Landschaft bestehen aus Bergen und Plateaus.

Landeinwärts sind die Fjells begrenzt durch steile Täler, die in der Eiszeit entstanden sind. Ihre Wände fallen senkrecht ab in die Fjorde. Nach den Worten des norwegischen Romanciers Sigurd Hoel sehen diese einzigartigen Täler aus, als seien sie von Kobolden in die Landschaft gepflügt worden. Langgestreckte Seen ziehen sich durch diese Täler, während sich auf den Landflächen hoch über ihnen die Überbleibsel der Sommerweiden ausbreiten, die einst ein typisches Merkmal der Landwirtschaft dort waren. Jedes der Täler – wie Hallingdal, Gudbrandsdal, Österdal, Setesdal und Numedal – ist so einzigartig und unvergleichlich wie jeder Fjord.

Die geschützten Gebiete im Landesinnern, besonders im Osten Norwegens, sind dicht bewaldet. Kiefer und Fichte überwiegen, die Birke ist weitverbreitet. Ein Gürtel aus Eichen und Buchen erstreckt sich an der Südküste, und in höheren Zonen, unterhalb der Baumgrenze, wachsen Zwergbirken und Weiden. Das Forstmuseum in Österdal bei Elverum, idyllisch am Ostufer des Glommen-Stroms gelegen, vermittelt einen hervorragenden Überblick über die Ökologie und Wirtschaft dieser Waldgebiete über Generationen hinweg. Im Osten ist auch der fruchtbarste Boden für die Landwirtschaft, besonders im Umkreis von Norwegens größtem See, dem Mjøsen-See. Zur Erntezeit ist er umrahmt von leuchtendgelben Getreidefeldern. Robuste, mittelalterliche Kirchen und Gehöfte, von denen einige zu den größten des Landes zählen, bezeugen den früh begründeten Wohlstand der Landwirtschaft in diesem Gebiet. Auch die Südküste und die Gegend um den Trondheimfjord sind mit ergiebigen landwirtschaftlichen Flächen gesegnet. Dennoch: weniger als vier Prozent der Fläche Norwegens ist landwirtschaftlich genutzt. Etwa zwanzig. Prozent der Landesfläche sind ertragreiches Waldgebiet.

Trotz seiner nördlichen Lage auf der Erdkugel herrscht in Norwegen ein milderes Klima als in anderen Ländern gleicher geographischer Breite. Das liegt am Golf-Strom und an den Westwinden, die das norwegische Wetter maßgeblich beeinflussen.

Die verhältnismäßig milden Temperaturen haben natürlich ihren Einfluß auf die Pflanzenwelt. Bäume, Sträucher und andere Pflanzen, die sonst nur in gemäßigten Klimazonen zu finden sind, wachsen wohl nirgends weiter nördlich als in Norwegen. Die Rotbuchen in den Gartenanlagen rund um den Trondheimfjord sowie die Rhododendronstauden, die in den Parks von Bergen gedeihen, veranschaulichen das. Auch vom Meeresleben muß gesprochen werden. Das relativ warme Seewasser mit starken Gezeiten und Strömungen bleibt auch im Winter eisfrei und bietet Lebensraum für eine reiche Pflanzen- und Tierwelt. Die Vielfalt von Meerestieren und – gewächsen, ihre Heimat, und der Charakter der Wirtschaft, die sich darauf stützt, werden im Fischereimuseum von Bergen den Besuchern nahegebracht. Seevögel sind ein wesentlicher Bestandteil der Küstenfauna. In Schwärmen bevölkern sie die phantastischen Vogelfelsen entlang den nördlichen Teilen der Küste.

Dadurch, daß Norwegen sich über so viele Breitengrade hinweg erstreckt und daß die Landschaft eine reliefartige Oberfläche mit vielen Höhen und Tiefen hat, ist das Klima von Region zu Region sehr verschieden. Gleichzeitig liegt Norwegen in der atlantischen Tiefdruckzone, weshalb das Wetter sehr unbeständig ist. Wetternachrichten im Radio dauern dementsprechend lange. In einigen Teilen West-Norwegens wurden die höchsten Niederschlagswerte ganz Europas gemessen. Man könnte diese Gegend "Land der Regenschirme" nennen, denn sogar im Winter fällt eher Regen als Schnee. Im Gegensatz dazu erfährt Ost-Norwegen wärmere und sonnigere Sommer, dafür aber auch kältere Winter. Im Windschatten westlich der Berge gibt es Täler wie Gudbrandsdal und Ottadal, die künstlich bewässert werden müssen, um eine ausreichende Ernte zu sichern. Die Länge Norwegens macht sich auch im deutlich wahrnehmbaren, jahreszeitlichen Rhythmus von Tageslicht und Dunkelheit bemerkbar. In ganz Norwegen sind die Sommernächte recht hell, und die Bewohner der nördlichen Landesteile wie Troms, Finmark und Nordland können sich im Sommer an der Mitternachtssonne erfreuen. Im Winter dagegen kennt man Mørketiden – die Zeit, während der es nur in den Mittagsstunden hell wird. Bei klarem Himmel zieht sich das nördliche Polarlicht wie ein bläulich leuchtender Vorhang durch die Dunkelheit der Nacht. Es ist in Nord-Norwegen häufiger wahrzunehmen als irgendwo sonst und ist Gegenstand eines wissenschaftlichen Forschungsprojektes eines Instituts in Tromsø. Die Wiederkehr des Sonnenlichts nach der Finsternis des Winters ist eine willkommene Gelegenheit für Festlichkeiten, und die Kinder im Norden freuen sich immer wieder auf die Feiern anläßlich der Tages der Sonnen-Wiederkehr.

Für die großen Vorteile, die Norwegen dank seines angenehmen Klimas und der ungewöhnlichen Beschaffenheit seiner Landschaft genießt, muß es manchmal einen hohen Preis zahlen. In schneereichen Wintern droht die Gefahr mächtiger Lawinen, die die Gebirgshänge hinunterdonnern, und ununterbrochener Regen kann Schlammlawinen oder Überflutungen verursachen.

Die ausgedehnten Gebirgszüge sind mittlerweile zu nationalen Erholungsgebieten erklärt worden, und von der Schulzeit an wird allen Norwegern beigebracht, die Berge und Schluchten zu respektieren und zu schützen. Im Winter wie im Sommer erhalten die Landesbürger Anweisungen, wie sie sich im Falle von Naturkatastrophen verhalten sollten. Und Wehrpflichtige, die gerade ihren Militärdienst ableisten, müssen sich anstrengenden Übungen unter winterlichen Bedingungen unterziehen. Ein anderes, aber nicht weniger ernstzunehmendes Umweltbewußtsein wird von denen erwartet, die es zur Erholung an die Seen zieht. Der Sommer ist die ideale Jahreszeit für Hochland-Wanderungen. Dafür wurde ein Netz von Wanderwegen geschaffen, die von einer Berghütte zur anderen führen. Die Hütten werden von der jahrhundertalten Fremdenverkehrsvereinigung des Landes unterhalten. Der Sommer ist auch die Zeit der Bergsteiger (ein Sport, der zum Teil in Norwegen seine Wurzeln hat) und der Segelfreunde (wobei die Kunst des Bootsbaus immer noch mit äußerster Präzision ausgeübt wird). Im Winter kommen natürlich die Skiläufer zum Zuge. Bis in unser Jahrhundert hinein waren die Ski im Winter für die Fortbewegung unersetzlich. Wie das Wort "Ski" schon verrät, wurde das Skifahren in Norwegen geboren. Das Skimuseum in Oslo gibt auf einfache aber anschauliche Art und Weise einen Einblick in die Geschichte dieses Sports. Noch immer ist das Skifahren als Sport vor allem bei Männern sehr beliebt. Doch seit dem letzten Jahrhundert finden auch Frauen mehr und mehr Gefallen an dieser Sportart.

Erst in den letzten Jahrzehnten hat Norwegen ein wohldurchdachtes Netz von Transportverbindungen bekommen. Moderne Ausrüstung und Ingenieurwissen sind gewissenhaft beim Autobahn- und Flugplatzbau sowie bei ihrer Instandhaltung eingesetzt worden, besonders dann, wenn es darum ging, die Durchquerung von unwegsamen Gebieten zu erleichtern. Wahrscheinlich kommen in Norwegen mehr Straßentunnel auf jeden Einwohner als in irgendeinem anderen Land. Der längste Straßentunnel ist 11 km lang, führt von Gudvanger nach Flaam (beim Sognefjord) und wird 1991 eröffnet. Auf sein heutiges Straßennetz kann Norwegen stolz sein. Auf der E 6-Route ist zum Beispiel nur noch ein Fährübergang übriggeblieben, der über den Tysfjord in Nordland führt. Zahlreiche Fähren verkehren in den Fjorden und verbinden auf der gesamten Küstenlänge Inseln und Festland miteinander. Durch den Flugverkehr ist das Leben für viele im Lande wesentlich einfacher geworden. Außerdem wurde die Wirtschaft angekurbelt und die Aufgabenerfüllung von Wohlfahrtsorganisationen wesentlich erleichtert. Spezialkliniken können nun zusammengelegt werden, weil in Notfällen Rettungshubschrauber auch abgelegene Siedlungen erreichen können. Auch für den Bau und die Wartung von Hochspannungskabeln und Telefonleitungen in schwer zugänglichem Gelände hat sich der Hubschrauber als wahrer Segen erwiesen.

Das Nationalbewußtsein Norwegens ist ein noch neues Phänomen. Im Jahre 1906, als Norwegen sich von der schwedischen Krone lossagte und zum unabhängigen Staat wurde, war der Gemeinschaftssinn der Bevölkerung nicht besonders stark entwickelt. In jedem Tal und an jedem Fjord führten die Bewohner ihr eigenes Leben. Unterschiedliche Dialekte, Bräuche, Folkore, Baustile, Mode und Aberglauben wurden in der Isolation erhalten und gepflegt. Einen Eindruck vom Ausmaß dieser Unterschiede kann man in den örtlichen und regionalen Volkskundemuseen erhalten. Das Volkskundemuseum auf Bygdøy in Oslo und eines in Ost-Norwegen sind hervorragende Beispiele. Paradoxerweise entstanden die Museen zur gleichen Zeit zu der Norwegen sich seiner Rückständigkeit und relativen Armut bewußt wurde. Das war in der Epoche der Industrialisierung West-Europas, als ein Strom von Auswanderern, die in der "Neuen Welt" ihr Glück versuchen wollten, Norwegen verließ. Auch die Glanzzeit der Vaterlandspoeten fiel in diese Jahre. Sie breiteten romantischen Schein über nationale Gefühle und begeisterten sich nicht nur für die Landessprache "Landsmål", sondern förderten sie auch und lehnten damit die offizielle Sprache "Riksmål" ab, die ihre Wurzeln in der von Dänemark geprägten Zeit Norwegens hat. Einige weitsichtige Altertumsforscher, die dieser dänischen Periode eng verbunden waren, retteten die Ruinen einiger erhaltenswerter, mittelalterlicher Kirchen, bevor die Modernisten sie durch einheitlich mit weißem Turm und Schindeldächern versehene Gebäude ersetzen konnten.

Mittlerweile hatte Henrik Ibsen die Idee zu seinem abenteuerlichen "Peer Gynt" gehabt. Unförmige, haarige Kobolde (die weiblichen Angehörigen dieser Spezies hatten Hufe und Schwänze) und der Wassergeist hatten sichtbare Formen angenommen. Die Künstler der romantischen Schule brachten Bilder von idyllischen Landschaften und heimeligen Bauernstuben hervor. Das alles war, bevor die Industrialisten die modernen Realisten beeinflußten wie zum Beispiel im Falle von Edward Munch mit seinem Meisterwerk über die neurotische Stadtszene, oder auch Gustav Wigeland, dessen monumentale Darstellungen der Menschheit in Stein gehauen in Oslos Frogner-Park stehen.

Landwirtschaft, Waldwirtschaft, Fischerei und Bergbau sind heute als ehemals wichtigste Quelle zum Erwerb des Lebensunterhalts zugunsten von Industrien und Fabriken in den Hintergrund getreten. Die kleinen Bauernhöfe – die schon immer in Privatbesitz waren, da Norwegen nie ein Feudalsystem gekannt hat – haben sich fast alle auf Viehwirtschaft verlegt. Noch hört man das Bimmeln von Schafs- und Kuhglocken auf den Weiden und manchmal stößt man auf Ziegenherden, die in Straßentunneln Schutz suchen. Landwirtschaft wird stark subventioniert – und das ist auch nötig im arktischen Norwegen, wo die Wachstumsperiode nur fünf Monate lang ist. Manchmal werden Waldwirtschaft und Landwirtschaft gleichzeitig betrieben. Das ist besonders üblich in

Ost-Norwegen, wo die Waldbestände das Rohmaterial für die Papierfabriken rund um den Oslofjord liefern. Auch die Kombination von Fischerei und Landwirtschaft ist nicht selten. Professionelle Fischer gewinnen mit gemeinschaftlichen Fischdampfern und teurer Ausrüstung immer größere Anteile am Gesamtfang, aber die weniger gut ausgerüsteten Fischer beteiligen sich noch immer an den Frühlings-Kabeljaufängen vor den Lofoten und Frühlings-Heringfängen vor More und Romsdal im Westen. Lange Zeit war die Seehundjagd ein Nebenerwerb, während die uralte Wal-Industrie langsam abgebaut wurde. Andererseits werden Gewinne aus der Fischzucht immer mehr zur Aufbesserung des Einkommens aus der Landwirtschaft benötigt. Zum Beispiel gibt es in Norwegen nicht weniger als 700 Lachszuchtbetriebe. Fuchs- und Nerzzucht sind ähnlich lohnenswert. Rentierzucht wird vor allem in den Bezirken von Troms und Finmark betrieben und bleibt ein Beruf für Fachleute. Die zahmen Herden wandern mit den Jahreszeiten. Die Zahl der Herden beläuft sich auf etwa 200 000. Die ethnisch eigenständigen Lappen, die sich selbst "Samen" nennen, bestreiten ihren Lebensunterhalt heute als Bauern, Fischer oder Rentierhüter, wobei die letzte Berufsgruppe die kleinst eist.

Seitdem Schmiede gegen Ende der Eisenzeit aus örtlich abgebautem Erz und Holzkohle die Ausrüstung der Wikinger herstellten, war das Metallhandwerk den Fachleuten vorbehalten. Durch die königlichen Silberminen hallen heute die Schritte von Touristen anstatt die der Minenarbeiter, die mehrere Generationen lang hier gearbeitet haben. Die Kupfererzvorräte aus den Minen des Røros Vidda und des arktischen Kaffjords sind seit langem erschöpft, allerdings wird dort noch immer Schwefelkies gefördert. Das Weltmonopol der Kobalt-Minen von Hangfoss mußte aufgegeben werden, als die damalige I.G. Farben chemische Farbstoffe auf den Markt brachte. Aber Vorkommen wichtiger Erze wie Bleierz und Titan werden noch abgebaut, während gleichzeitig riesige Tagebauanlagen auf dem Südufer des Varangerfjords geringe Mengen von Eisenerz hervorbringen. Ein anderer Bodenschatz als Erz verhilft Norwegen heute zu Reichtum: unter den westeuropäischen Nationen ist Norwegen der Löwenanteil an Öl- und Erdgasvorkommen zugefallen. Und Geologen haben versichert, daß außerhalb der Nordsee-Bohrfelder, vor der Nordwest-Küste und im Barents-Meer, noch reichliche Reserven vorhanden sind. Die technischen Schwierigkeiten bei der Ausdehnung des Fördergebietes in unruhigere Teile des Meeres stellen kaum noch ein Problem dar. Was noch aussteht ist eine Einigung mit der Sowjetunion über den Verlauf der Grenzen im arktischen Meeresgebiet. Bis zur Lösung dieses politischen Problems beschränken sich Norwegen und die UdSSR darauf, Kohle auf dem Svalbard-Archipel abzubauen, wo 1500 Norweger pro Jahr etwa 500 000 Tonnen Kohle fördern.

Nur ein geringer Anteil von Norwegens Energieverbrauch wird allerdings aus Bodenschätzen gedeckt. Der Grund dafür ist klar: Klima und Beschaffenheit des Landes machen es leicht, große Mengen von elektrischer Energie mit Hilfe von Wasserkraft zu erzeugen. Nachdem Großanlagen zur Stromgewinnung und leistungsfähige Stromleitungen für große Entfernungen entstanden waren, wurde der Strom aus Wasserkraftwerken zu einem wichtigen Bestandteil des norwegischen Lebens. Der Dichter Bjørnstjerne Bjørnson lebte lange genug, um "die stürzenden Ströme... zu Licht verwandelt" noch erleben und beschreiben zu können. Während die bestgeeigneten Stellen im Lande für die Stromgewinnung nutzbar gemacht wurden, wurden gleichzeitig immer perfektere Systeme entworfen, um aus Wasserkraft Energie gewinnen zu können. Hochland-Seen wurden miteinander verbunden und an die Ränder der Plateaus geleitet, wo der höchste Wasserstand erreicht werden konnte. Längst sind nicht alle Möglichkeiten ausgeschöpft, aber das Eindämmen von Wasserfällen wird zunehmend beschränkt. Konservative sowie die Förderer des Tourismus kritisieren die Planer. Die Auseinandersetzungen über Voringfoss, der über den Rand des Hardangervidda in die Tiefe des Måbodal-Tals stürzt, sind ein gutes Beispiel.

Anfangs war Strom aus Wasserkraftwerken verhältnismäßig billig, und Industriezweige wie die Aluminiumverarbeitung profitierten wesentlich davon. Inzwischen ist der Energiebedarf so groß geworden, daß es zu saisonalen oder regionalen Engpässen in der Energieversorgung kommen kann. Am größten ist die Nachfrage gewöhnlich im Winter, wenn gleichzeitig der Wasserfluß abnimmt. Hauptenergieverbraucher sind die elektrometallurgische und die elektrochemische Industrie. Dazu gehört auch der Chemie-Gigant "Norsk Hydro" mit seinen riesigen Werksanlagen auf Herøya bei Porsgrunn. Das staatseigene Eisen- und Stahlwerk Mo i Ranas in Nordland wurde als Wirtschaftsförderungsmaßnahme in einem Gebiet hoher Arbeitslosigkeit und industrieller Unterentwicklung aufgebaut und ist bei Røssaga an das Energieversorgungsnetz angeschlossen. Ein Schwachpunkt in der norwegischen Wirtschaft sind die von einer einzigen Industriebranche abhängigen Kommunen. Über 70 gibt es davon in Norwegen, und alle unterliegen völlig der Marktsituation. Dementsprechend stagnieren einige Produktionszweige, andere verzeichnen einen Rückgang, was wiederum sozialen Problemen Auftrieb verleiht. Trotzdem geraten Gesellschaft und Wirtschaft nicht so häufig in Konflikt wie man erwarten könnte, dank der Tatsache, daß die Einkünfte aus dem Ölgeschäft oft für großzügige Hilfeleistungen verwandt werden. Jedoch wirft das ein weiteres Problem auf, weil die Ölausfuhr 50 Prozent von Norwegens Gesamtexport ausmacht, womit das Exportgeschäft zur Hälfte vom unbeständigen Weltmarkt abhängig ist. Aber all das sind Überlegungen, die dem Besucher Norwegens nicht sofort in den Sinn kommen.

Vielmehr wird sich der Tourist bereitwillig dem Zauber des Landes ergeben. Die gewaltigen Gegensätze des Lebensraumes der Norweger sind eine anziehungskräftige Touristenattraktion. Auf der einen Seite die beschaulichen, kultivierten Terrains, die im Sommer an den Garten von Eden erinnern (und im Winter an die Heimat des Weihnachtsmannes). Tatsächlich gibt es eine Siedlung mit dem Namen "Paradies". Sie ist eine von Bergens Vororten. Das Gegenstück dazu ist "Holle", ein kleines Dorf im Bezirk von Trondelag. Landesbesuchern wird sehr schnell auffallen, daß Norwegen ein Land ist, das mehr als die meisten anderen Jung und Alt gleichermaßen gerecht wird. Für Kinder ist Norwegen ein Abenteuerland, besonders, da die meisten Familien eine See- oder Berghütte besitzen, oder zumindest Zugang dazu haben. Den Angehörigen der älteren Generation gibt es ein gutes Gefühl zu wissen, daß nur in Schweden und Island die Menschen eine ähnlich hohe Lebenserwartung haben. Und für Touristen aus reich bevölkerten Ländern ist es eine Freude, auf ein Land zu treffen, wo es nach den Worten von Gertrude Stein "mehr Plätze gibt, wo keiner ist, als Plätze, wo einer ist."

Zweifellos haben die Weite des Landes und der See Selbständigkeit und Unabhängigkeit der Norweger gefördert, Eigenschaften, die für die Figuren in Ibsen's Werken charakteristisch sind. Am stärksten kamen solche Charakterzüge in den Kriegswiderstands-bewegungen zum Ausdruck. Genausogut könnten sie für die Volksabstimmung zur Ablehnung der EG-Mitgliedschaft verantwortlich sein. Und auch die Tatsache, daß die meisten Norweger vom Lande kommen und sich immer wieder dort hingezogen fühlen, hängt mit diesen Charaktereigenschaften zusammen. Andererseits kann das Wissen darüber erklären helfen, warum die meisten Norweger sich so leicht an den einfachen Dingen des Lebens erfreuen können und den Gefallen daran auch auf andere übertragen können. Mit Gewißheit werden diejenigen Besucher am meisten von Norwegen haben, die an der unbeschwerten Heiterkeit von Volksbräuchen, -gesängen und -tänzen teilhaben können, die bäuerliche Handwerkskunst bewundern, die ein evokatives Musikstück von Grieg zu schätzen wissen, und die immer wieder berührt sind von den patriotischen Festen am 17. Mai (Tag der Verfassungsgründung), mit ihren Prozessionen, Historienspielen, Festreden und Fahnenschwenkern. Selten erscheinen Zeitgeist und Geist eines Volkes in solcher Übereinstimmung wie in Norwegen. Ist es wirklich nur ein glücklicher Zufall, daß dieses reizvolle Land sich eine der Welt melodischsten Nationalhymnen ausgesucht hat, deren Text zu singen einen nicht in Verlegenheit bringt? Ja vi elsker dette landet – Ja, wir lieben dieses Land.

Foregående side: Parti fra Oslo havn med skoleskipet Christian Radich. I bakgrunnen Akershus Festning. Denne side, under: Turistbåter på havna, nederst: fra Stortorget med Domkirken, og til høyre: glimt fra Studenterlunden. Neste side: Stortingsbygningen.

Previous page: part of Oslo harbour showing 'Christian Radich' with, in the background, Akershus Castle. Below: sightseeing from the harbour. Bottom: Market Square and the cathedral and (right and below right) Studenterlunden park. Facing page: the Storting (parliament).

Vorhergehende Seite: Teilansicht des Hafens von Oslo mit dem Schulschiff "Christian Radich". Im Hintergrund : Die Festung Akershus. Diese Seite, unten: Aussicht vom Hafen. Ganz unten: Marktplatz und Kathedrale. Rechts: Studenterlunden-Park. Nächste Seite: das Parlamentsgebäude "Storting".

Forrige side: Slottet i Oslo. Denne side øverst: Rådhuset i Oslo en sommerdag – og i nattbelysning. Nederst: Fra populære Aker Brygge.

Facing page: the Royal Palace, Oslo. Left and below: Oslo City Hall by day and by night. Bottom left and right: the "in" place, Aker Brygge.

Links: Der Königliche Palast, Oslo. Oben: Das Rathaus von Oslo, im Sommer und bei Nacht. Unten: Ein beliebtes Ziel, Aker Brygge.

Øverst til venstre: Utsikt mot Slottet. Over: Natt over Stortorget, og nederst til venstre: Aker Brygge og Rådhuset. Til venstre: Kongens Garde har vaktskifte utenfor Slottet. Neste side: En kald vinterkveld på islagte Oslo havn med restaurant – og hotellskip ved kai under Akershus Festning.

Top left: view of the Palace. Above: Market Square and the cathedral by night. Far left: Aker Brygge and City Hall. Left: changing the palace guard. Facing page: ice in Oslo harbour on a winter night, and a restaurant/hotel ship berthed by Akershus Castle.

Oben links: Blick auf den Palast. Oben rechts: Marktplatz und Kathedrale bei Nacht. Ganz links: Aker Brygge und Rathaus. Links Wachwechsel am Palast. Nächste Seite: Der vereiste Hafen von Oslo in einer Winternacht, ein Hotel-Schiff hat vor Akershus angelegt.

Billedhuggeren Gustav Vigeland (1869-1943) er kunstneren som skapte de 192 skulpturene som viser menneskets vandring fra fødsel til død. De er plassert i det gigantiske Vigelandsanlegget i Frognerparken.

These pages: the artistic might of Gustav Vigeland (1869-1943) features 192 sculptures depicting man from birth to death, all in the splendour of the Vigeland Park, Frogner.

Das künstlerische Vermächtnis Gustav Vigelands (1869-1943). 192 Skulpturen im herrlichen Vigeland-Park (Frogner) zeigen den Menschen, von der Geburt bis zum Tod.

På Bygdøy ligger flere av hovedstadens museer: Ved Frammuseet med Fridtjof Nansens pol-skip "Fram", ligger Roald Amundsens "Gjøa", (helt til venstre). Sjøfartsmuseet med bl.a. Osebergskipet (til venstre og under) og Norsk Folkemuseum (nede til venstre). Neste side: Skoleskipet "Christian Radich" på Oslo havn.

Many of Oslo's museums are on Bygdøy. By the Fram museum, with Fridtjof Nansen's "Fram", is Roald Amundsen's "Gjøa", (far left). An authentic Viking ship (left) is featured at the Maritime Museum (bottom). Bottom left: the Norwegian Folk Museum, and (facing page) the cadet ship "Christian Radich", berthed in Oslo harbour.

Viele von Oslos Museen befinden sich auf Bygdøy. Neben dem "Fram"-Museum, wo unter anderem Fridtjof Nansens "Fram" untergebracht ist, steht Roald Amundsens "Gjøa, (oben links). Ein echtes Wikinger-Schiff im Seefahrtsmuseum (links). Das norwegische Volkskundemuseum, (unten links). Nächste Seite: Das Kadetten-Schiff "Christian Radich" im Osloer Hafen.

Norsk Folkemuseum har ca. 170 gamle hus, flere gårdstun, en stavkirke fra Gol i Hallingdal samt over 170.000 gjenstander fra hele landet. Neste side: Akershus Slott og Festning fra ca. 1300-årene. Nederst til høyre: Parti fra Holmenkollen Skiarena som også er et populært sted om sommeren.

This page: 170 historic buildings are sited in the Norwegian Folk Museum. These include rural dwellings and a stave church from Gol in Hallingdal, plus 170,000 items from all over Norway. Facing page: (left and top right) Akershus castle, dating from about 1300. Bottom right: the Homenkollen ski jump, popular in summer as well as in winter.

170 historische Gebäude kann man im norwegischen Volkskundemuseum bestaunen, unter anderem Bauernhäuser und eine Stabkirche aus Gol in Hallingdal. Außerdem 170 000 weitere Ausstellungsstücke aus ganz Norwegen. Nächste Seite: Die Festung Akershus aus der Zeit um 1300. Unten rechts: Die Homenkollen-Skischanze ist auch im Sommer gut besucht.

Fredrikstad. Den eldste delen, "Gamlebyen", (til høyre og nederst til høyre) er en godt bevart festningsby med bygninger fra 1700-tallet. Øverst til høyre: Krigsmonumentet fra 2. verdenskrig. Nederst til venstre: Parti fra gågaten i sentrum. Neste side: Den 1530 m lange Sandesundbroen ved Sarpsborg. Tunejordet i bakgrunnen.

Fredrikstad's "old town" still preserves its past as a fortress and its 18th century buildings (right and bottom right). Far right: a memorial from the World War II. Below: pedestrian precinct in the town centre. Facing page: the 1530m Sandesund bridge, Sarpsborg, with Tunejordet in the background.

Fredrikstad, diese alte Stadt pflegt ihre Vergangenheit als Festung und erhält ihre Gebäude aus dem 18. Jh. (oben rechts, unten rechts). Ganz rechts: Kriegerdenkmal. Unten: Fußgängerzone im Stadtzentrum. Nächste Seite: 1530 m lange Sandesund Brücke, Sarpsborg. Tunejordet im Hintergrund.

Forrige side: Øverst til venstre: Parken ved Moss kirke. Øverst til høyre: Hvalfangstmonumentet i Sandefjord. Nede til venstre: Vippefyret på Verdens Ende, Tjøme. Nede til høyre: Parti fra Byparken i Sandefjord. Denne side: Tønsberg, Norges eldste by. Parti fra havna, Domkirken i bakgrunnen, og nede til venstre: Parti fra Slottsfjellet med utsiktstårnet fra 1888. Under: Gammel veteranbåt i Vrengensundet.

Facing page: (top left) park by Moss church, (top right) whaling monument in Sandefjord, (bottom left) stone lighthouse on Tjøme and (bottom right) town park in Sandefjord. Left: the harbour and cathedral in Tønsberg, Norway's oldest town. Bottom left: Castle mount and the watchtower from 1888, and (below:) a veteran ship in Vrengensundet.

Vorhergehende Seite, oben links: Park an der Moss-Kirche. Oben rechts: Walfang-Denkmal in Sandefjord. Unten links: Leuchtturm bei Verdens Ende, Tjøme. Unten rechts: Stadtgarten in Sandefjord. Diese Seite: Tønsberg, Norwegens älteste Stadt, mit Hafen und Kathedrale. Unten links: Festungshügel mit Aussichtsturm von 1888. Darunter: Oldtimer-Schiff in Vrengensundet.

Under: Fra det idylliske Nevlunghavn. Til høyre: Parti fra Holmestrand med småbåthavna og Nordisk Aluminium A/S. Nederst: Den monumentale Minnehallen ved Stavern. Nederst til høyre: Stavern kirke fra 1756 og minnestøtten over falne fra siste krig. Neste side: Den populære Kjærstranda ved Larvik.
Below: The idyllic harbour of Nevlunghavn. Right: Holmestrand marina and Nordisk Aluminium's plant.
Bottom: Remembrance monument at Stavern. Bottom right: Stavern church, 1756, and war memorial
from World War II. Facing page: a popular beach, Kjærstranda, Larvik.
Unten: Der idyllische Hafen von Nevlunghavn. Oben rechts: Holmestrands Yachthafen mit Nordisk-Aluminium-Werk. Unten links: Denkmal bei Stavern. Unten rechts: Kirche in Stavern (1756) und Kriegerdenkmal. Nächste Seite: Ein beliebter Strand, Kjærstranda (Larvik).

Til venstre: Parti fra Larvik med danske-ferja "Peter Wessel" ved kai, og over: Larvik havn, like før start på en seilskip-regatta.

Facing page: view of Larvik and the ferry to Denmark "Peter Wessel". Above: Larvik harbour just before the start of a tall ship regatta.

Links: Blick auf Larvik und auf "Peter Wessel", die Fähre nach Dänemark. Oben: Der Hafen von Larvik kurz vor dem Start einer großen Schiffsregatte.

Oppe og nede til venstre: Utsikt over Brevik med Brevikbrua. I bakgrunnen Stathelle. Over: Parti fra Porsgrunn med blomstertorget. Til venstre: Fra Ibsenparken i Skien. Kirken i bakgrunnen. Til høyre: M/S Victoria på Kviteseidvatnet i Telemark.

Top left and far left: view of Brevik and Brevikbrua with Stathelle in the background. Above: Porsgrunn and the flower market. Left: Skien church from Ibsen's park. Facing page: M/S Victoria on Kviteseidvatnet in Telemark.

Ganz links, oben und unten: Blick auf Brevik und Brevikbrua. Im Hintergrund Stathelle. Oben: Porsgrunn mit Blumenmarkt. Links: Ibsens Park in Skien. Rechts: Die MS Victoria bei Kviteseidvatnet in Telemark.

Forrige side: Parti fra Kragerø, Øya i bakgrunnen. Denne side oppe og nede til venstre: Den idylliske havna i Risør, "den hvite by" ved Skagerak. Under til høyre er fra Kragerø's travle havn.

Facing page: part of Kragerø and the island, Øya. Left and below left: the idyllic harbour of Risør, "the white town" on the Skagerak. Below:

Kragerø's busy harbour.
Vorhergehende Seite: Teilansicht von Kragerø und der Insel Øya. Diese Seite, oben und unten links: Der idyllische Hafen von Risør, der "weißen Stadt" am Skagerak. Unten: Kragerøs geschäftiger Hafen.

Forrige side: Heddal Stavkirke, den største av stavkirkene fra 1300-tallet. Til venstre: Parti fra den gamle gruvebyen Kongsberg. Lågen i forgrunnen. Bak ruver kirken fra 1761. Under til venstre: Drammen med Bragernes Torv. Kirken i bakgrunnen. Under: Den enkle og stilrene Notodden kirke.

Facing page: Heddal stave church, Norway's largest 14th century stave church. Left: part of the historic mining town of Kongsberg, with its church dating from 1761. Below left: Drammen's market square. Below: the pure, unembellished lines of Notodden church.

Vorhergehende Seite: Stabkirche von Heddal, die größte Stabkirche aus dem 14. Jahrhundert. Links: Teilansicht der historischen Bergbaustadt Kongsberg mit Kirche aus 1761. Ganz links: Marktplatz von Drammen. Unten: Die stilgerechte Notodden Kirche.

Pollen i Arendal (over) er en populær havn om sommeren. Det samme kan sies om Grimstad (neste side), en koselig sørlandsby.

Both Pollen in Arendal (above) and the charming south coast town of Grimstad (facing page) are popular ports during the summer.

Pollen in Arendal (oben) ist im Sommer ein viel-besuchter Hafen. Grimstadt (rechts), eine reizvolle Stadt an der Südküste ist ähnlich beliebt.

Øverst: Brekkestø, en av Sørlandets perler. Øverst til høyre: Utsikt over Tvedestrands sjarmerende bebyggelse med Rådhuset i forgrunnen. Bildene nederst er fra Blindleia ved Lillesand. Neste side: Fra den livlige havna i den gamle seilskutebyen Lillesand.
Top: Brekkestø, one of the pearls of the south coast. Top right: Tvedestrand's snug dwellings, with the town hall in the foreground. Above and right: Blindleia off Lillesand. Facing page: the lively port in the former schooner town of Lillesand.
Oben: Brekkestø, eine "Perle" der Südküste. Oben rechts: Tvedestrand. Aussicht auf die gemütlichen Holzhäuser mit dem Rathaus im Vordergrund. Unten, links und rechts: Blindleia vor Lillesand. Nächste Seite: Der lebhafte ehemalige Schonerhafen von Lillesand.

Ved havna i Mandal står denne elegante statuen. Under: Utsikt over Kristiansand sentrum med Domkirken. Øverst til høyre: Idylliske Ravnedalen. Under til høyre: Parti fra Sjøsanden, Mandals største turistattraksjon. Neste side: Kristiansand sett fra fly.

Right: this elegant statue is found by the harbour in Mandal. Below: view of central Kristiansand and the cathedral. Far right: idyllic Ravnedalen. Below right: one of Mandal's attractions – Sjøsanden beach. Facing page: aerial view of Kristiansand.

Diese schöne Statue befindet sich im Hafen von Mandal. Unten: Blick auf das Stadtzentrum und die Kathedrale von Kristiansand. Oben rechts: Eine von Mandals Attraktionen, der Sjøsanden-Strand. Nächste Seite: Luftansicht von Kristiansand.

Til venstre: Norges oljeby Stavanger som har USA`s Houston, Texas, som vennskapsby, ligger lunt til.
– Breiavatnet i forgrunnen. Under: Domkirken fra middelalderen, og nederst, – og oppe til høyre
partier fra Vågen. Nederst, til høyre, fra et av gamle Stavangers smau.
Facing page: Norway's oil capital Stavanger, Houston's twin city, with Breiavatnet in the foreground.
Below: a cathedral from the Middle Ages. Right and bottom: part of Vågen. Bottom right: traditional
Stavanger.
Links: Norwegens Öl-Stadt Stavanger, Partnerstadt von Houston (Texas). Unten: Mittelalterliche
Kathedrale. Unten links und oben rechts: Teile von Vågen. Unten rechts: Das alte Stavanger.

Fra venstre, parti fra Gamle Stavanger,
– og interiør i Domkirken fra 11-1200-
årene. Nedenfor: Fisketorget og
blomstertorget ved Vågen. Dikteren
Alexander Kielland på sin sokkel
overvåker det hele. Til høyre:
Stavanger sett fra fly. Bybroa i
forgrunnen.

*Far left: the Old Town, and (left) the
interior of Stavanger's 12th-13th
century cathedral. Below left and
below: fish and flower market at
Vågen, where the poet Alexander
Kielland surveys life from his plinth.
Facing page: aerial view of Stavanger,
with the town bridge in the foreground.*

Links: Die Altstadtt,und Stavangers
Kathedrale (12/13. Jh) von innen.
Unten: Fisch- und Blumenmarkt von
Vågen. Der Dichter Alexander Kielland
beobachtet das Treiben vom Sockel
aus. Rechts: Luftbild von Stavanger, im
Vordergrund die Stadtbrücke.

Forrige side: Parti fra havna i den lille fiskebyen Skudeneshavn på Karmøy, vest for Stavanger. Til venstre: Utsyn over Jærens flate og frodige jordbruksområder. Nedenfor: Feistein Fyr, Jæren, i solnedgang, – og til høyre: Gamle Skudeneshavn, et av Norges mest særpregede byområder.

Facing page: part of the fisherman's harbour at Skudeneshavn on Karmøy, west of Stavanger. Left: Jæren, flat and fertile, an agricultural gem. Below left: sunset over Feistein lighthouse, Jæren. Below: one of Norway's most original places to live.

Vorhergehende Seite: Teilansicht vom Fischerdorf Skudeneshavn auf Karmøy, westlich von Stavanger. Links: Jærens flaches, ertragreiches Ackerland. Unten links: Sonnenuntergang am Feistein-Leuchtturm, Jæren. Unten: Eines von Norwegens frühesten Wohngebieten.

Den gamle fiske- og sjøfartsbyen Haugesund er vel nå blitt mere preget av verksted- og industrivirksomhet, men skipstrafikken er fremdeles livlig i Smedasundet. Til venstre: Minnestøtten på Haraldshaugen, og under: Rådhuset. Neste side: Parti fra Smedasundet, Haugesund.

The historic fishing and maritime town of Haugesund (these pages) is now an industrial centre, though shipping still thrives in Smedasundet. Below: the town hall and (below left) part of Smedasundet, Haugesund. Left: memorial on Haraldshaugen.

Die historische Fischerei- und Seefahrtstadt Haugesund ist heute eine Industriestadt, wenngleich die Schiffahrt in Smedasundet immer noch eine wichtige Rolle spielt. Links: Denkmal auf Haraldshaugen. Unten: Rathaus. Unten links: Teilansicht von Smedasundet, Haugesund.

Bergen, fra år 1070, har mye fin gammel bebyggelse. Bryggen ved Vågen (oppe til venstre) er blant bevaringsverdige historiske minner og Håkonshallen (nedenfor) er fra byens storhetstid ca. 1260. Til venstre: Edvard Griegs hjem "Trollhaugen" og over: Utsikt over torget. Til høyre: Fra Vågen med Bryggen og skoleskipet "Statsraad Lehmkuhl".

Bergen, founded in 1070, has many fine buildings. "Bryggen" (top left) is part of Hanseatic trading history. "Håkonshallen" (far left) dates from the city's prominent period ca. 1260. Left: Edvard Grieg's dwelling "Trollhaugen". Above: view of the fish market. Right: "Bryggen" and cadet ship "Statsraad Lehmkuhl" from Vågen.

Im 1070 gegründeten Bergen gibt es viele sehenswerte Gebäude. Die Kaianlagen (oben links) sind Teil der hanseatischen Handelsgeschichte. "Håkonshallen" Burg (unten) stammt aus der berühmten Zeit der Stadt um 1260. Links: Edvard Griegs Wohnhaus "Trollhaugen". Oben: Blick auf den Fischmarkt. Rechts: Die Kaianlagen mit dem Schulschiff "Statsraad Lehmkuhl", aus Vågen.

Forrige side: Utsikt over Bergen med Vågen. I bakgrunnen Askøy. Til venstre: Bergen er en vakker by også når solen har gått ned.
Under: 2 av byens attraksjoner – Ulriksbanen som går opp til Ulrikens topp – vel 600 m.o.h., og Fløybanen som går opp til toppen av det 300 m høye Fløyfjellet.

Facing page: Bergen and Vågen, with Askøy in the background. Left: the beauty of Bergen at night. Below left and below: two of Bergen's attractions: the cablecar up to Ulriken (600m), and the mountain railway to Fløyen (300m).

Vorhergehende Seite: Bergen und die Vågen. Im Hintergrund Askøy. Bergen ist auch nachts einen Besuch wert. Unten: Zwei von Bergens Attraktionen, die Bergbahn nach Ulriken (600 m hoch) und die Seilbahn nach Fløyen (300 m).

Under: Utsikt over Nærøydalen med Stalheim Hotell, Jordalsnuten og veien ut til Gudvangen. Helt til høyre: Utsikt over Måbødalen med Vøringfossen i forgrunnen. Neste side: Til fjells fra Voss kommer man lett og raskt med svevebanen Hangursbanen og med stolheis til over 800 m.o.h.

Below: Nærøydalen and the Stalheim Hotel, and the road to Gudvangen. Far right: Måbødalen with the famous Vøringfossen falls in the foreground. Facing page: the chair-lift at Voss speedily takes visitors to 800m.

Unten: Nærøydalen und das Stalheim Hotel mit Sicht auf die Straße nach Gudvangen. Unten rechts: Måbödalen mit den berühmten Vöringfossen Wasserfäll im Vordergrund. Nächste Seite: Der Sessellift bei Voss bringt einen bequem und schnell auf 800 Meter Höhe.

Over, blomstrer frukttrœrne i Ulvik,
Hardanger. Over til høyre: Ved fergestedet
Vangsnes står denne 12 m høye
Fridtjovstatuen på sin 15 m høye sokkel og
skuer utover Sognefjorden. Til høyre: Den
gamle Borgund Stavkirke i Sogn, – og parti
fra Ullensvang i Hardanger. Neste side:
Unge piker i sine vakre Hardanger-bunader.

Above: apple blossom in Ulvik, Hardanger.
Above right: the Fridtjov statue towers over
25m above the ferry terminus at Vangsnes,
Sognefjorden. Right: Borgund stave
church in Sogn, and (far right) Ullensvang in
Hardanger. Facing page: young girls
pictured in their delightful national costume
– (Hardanger).

Oben: Apfelbaumblüte in Ulvik, Hardanger.
Oben rechts: Die Fridtjov-Statue mehr als
25 Meter über der Fährstation bei
Vangsnes im Sognefjord. Rechts: Die
Borgund Stabkirche in Sogn, und
Ullensvang in Hardanger. Nächste Seite:
Junge Mädchen in ihren hübschen
Trachtenkleidern – (Hardanger).

Øverst: Veien over Sognefjell en sommerdag. Øverst til høyre: Båttur til Nigaardsbreen, en arm av Jostedalsbreen. Over: Parti fra Balestrand i Sogn. Til høyre: Sommerdag på Sognefjellet med snødekte vidder og fjell. Neste side: Fra idylliske Svœrefjorden i Sogn.
Top: the road across Sognefjell in summer. Top right: boat trips to Nigaards glacier, an arm of Jostedals glacier. Above: view from Balestrand, Sogn. Right: the snow-capped Sognefjell mountains in summer. Facing page: the idyllic Svœrefjorden in Sogn.
Oben links: Die Straße durch das Sognefjell im Sommer. Rechts: Bootsfahrt zum Nigaard-Gletscher, ein Nebenarm des Jostedal-Gletschers. Oben: Ausblick von Balestrand, Sogn. Rechts: Die schneebedeckten Berge des Sognefjell im Sommer. Nächste Seite: Der idyllische Svœrefjord in Sogn.

Lengst til venstre: Våronn i Stardalen, Jostedalsbreen i bakgrunnen. Nedenfor: "Gode venner" ved Kjøsnesfjord. Til venstre: Småpiker i nasjonaldrakter ved Jølstravannet. Under: Parti fra Høyset i Stardalen mot Fonn. Neste side: Turistskip og bilferge ved Gudvangen i den vakre Nærøyfjorden.

Far left: spring sowing in Stardalen, with the Jostedal glacier in the background. Bottom left: friends, Kjøsnesfjord. Left: girls in national costume, Jølstravannet. Below: view from Høyset towards Fonn. Facing page: cruise ship and car ferry in the beautiful Nærøyfjord.

Oben links: Frühlingssaat in Stardalen. Im Hintergrund der Jostedal- Gletscher. Unten links: Zwei gute Freunde, Kjøsnesfjord. Links: Mädchen in Landestrachten bei Jølstravannet. Unten: Ausblick von Høyset nach Fonn. Rechts: Seekreuzer und Autofähre im schönen Nærøyfjord.

Over til venstre: Hestetrille på brua over Briksdalsfossen. Under: Parti fra veien Byrkjelo-Skei. Eggenipa i bakgrunnen. Over: Briksdalsbreen, en arm av Jostedalsbreen. Til høyre: Ved Briksdalsfossen med breen i bakgrunnen.
Above left: a horse and trap cross the Briksdals falls. Left: view of Eggenipa, on the Byrkjelo-Skei road. Above: Briksdalsbreen, an arm of the Jostedals glacier. Facing page: Briksdals falls carrying the glacial meltwater.
Oben links: Pferd und Wagen überqueren die Briksdal-Wasserfälle. Links: Blick auf Eggenipa an der Byrkjelo-Skei-Straße. Oben: Der Briksdal-Gletscher, ein Nebenarm des Jostedal-Gletschers. Rechts: Das Schmelzwasser der Gletscher rauscht die Briksdal-Fälle hinunter.

Over: Fisketur på Oldevatnet mellom Olden og Briksdalen. Til
høyre: Ved en laksetrapp i Oldenelva. "Cesilie-kruna" (1717 m)
oppe til høyre.

Above: fishing in Oldevatnet, between Olden and Briksdalen.
Right: a salmon trap on the Olden river. "Cesilie-kruna" (1717m)
dominates the skyline on the right.

Oben: Fischfang in Oldevatnet, zwischen Olden und Briksdalen.
Rechts: Eine Lachsfangvorrichtung am Olden-Fluß. Rechts im
Bild beherrscht der 1717 m hohe "Cesilie-kruna" den Horizont.

72

Forrige side: Parti fra Hjelledalen med fjellene ved Strynsvatnet i bakgrunnen. Over: Utsikt fra Videseter, ned Hjelledalen. Til høyre øverst: Parti fra Strynselva. Nederst: Fra Loen-vatnet, Kjenndalsbreen i bakgrunnen.
Facing page: Hjelledalen with, in the background, the mountains near Lake Strynsvatnet. Above: view from Videseter down Hjelledalen. Above right: the River Strynselva. Right: Loenvatnet reflects the Kjenndals glacier.
Links: Hjelledalen und im Hintergrund die Berge beim See Strynsvatnet. Oben: Ausblick von Videseter auf Hjelledalen. Oben rechts: Der Fluß Strynselva. Unten rechts: Im Loenvatnet spiegelt sich der Kjenndal-Gletscher.

Over: Parti fra Loenvatn, Kjenndalen i bakgrunnen. Til høyre: Ved Loen kirke, "Skåla" 1848 m i bakgrunnen.

Above: Loenvatnet with Kjenndalen in the background. Facing page: Loen church, dominated by "Skåla" (1848m), in the background.

Oben: Loenvatnet mit Kjenndalen im Hintergrund. Rechts: Die Loen-Kirche, überragt vom "Skåla" (1848 m) im Hintergrund.

Til venstre: Måløy med den 1224 m lange Måløybrua i forgrunnen. Over: Aftenstemning på Stadlandet.

Facing page: Måløy, with the 1224m-long Måløy bridge. Above: evening tranquility at Stadlandet.

Links: Målöy mit der 1224 m langen Målöy-Brucke. Oben: Abendruhe bei Stadlandet.

Forrige side: Fisketur på Gjende.Til venstre: Utsikt over Gjende og Gjendesheim i Jotunheimen.Under: Lom Stavkirke, og nederst til venstre Vågå Stavkirke, og til høyre: Pillarguristøtten ved Otta i Gudbrandsdalen.
Facing page: fishing on Gjende. Left: view across Gjende and Gjendesheim in Jotunheimen. Below: Lom Stave Church, and (bottom left) Vågå Stave Church. Bottom: an ancient war memorial in Otta, Gudbrandsdalen.
Ganz links: Fischfang auf dem Gjende. Oben links: Blick über Gjende See und Gjendesheim im Gebirge Jotunheimen. Unten: Lom Stabkirche. Ganz unten links: Stabkirche von Vågå. Unten rechts: Ein altes Kriegerdenkmal in Otta, Gudbrandsdalen.

Forrige side: Hjuldamperen "Skibladner" på Mjøsa. Øverst til venstre: Eidsvollsbygningen, hvor grunnloven ble proklamert 17. mai l814, og til høyre: Parti fra Lillehammer sett fra Vingnes. Til venstre: Domkirkeruinene ved Hamar, og over: Småbåthavn ved Vingnesbrua mot Lillehammer.

Facing page: the paddle steamer "Skibladner" on Mjøsa. Top left: Eidsvoll, where the Constitution was signed in 1814. Top: Lillehammer from Vingnes. Left: cathedral ruins at Hamar. Above: marina at Vingnesbrua, Lillehammer.

Vorhergehende Seite: Schaufelraddampfer auf dem Mjøsa. Oben links: Eidsvoll, wo am 17. Mai 1814 die Verfassung unterzeichnet wurde. Oben rechts: Lillehammer, von Vingnes aus. Links: Ruine einer Kathedrale bei Hamar. Oben: Yachthafen bei Vingnesbrua, Lillehammer.

Forrige side: Vinternatt i Rondane. Atnasjøen i forgrunnen, og i bakgrunnen fra venstre: Storronden 2142 m – Rondeslottet 2178 m – Høgronden 2114 m. Denne side til venstre: Måneskinn over Dovrefjell. Nederst til venstre: Elven Store Ula mot Rondeslottet og Storronden. Under: Vinternatt i bergstaden Røros.

Facing page: winter night in Rondane with, in the foreground, Atnasjøen and, in the background, left to right: Storronden, 2142m, Rondeslottet, 2178m and Høgronden, 2114m. Left: Dovrefjell in the moonlight. Below left: the Store Ula river with Rondeslottet and Storronden, and (below) a winter night in the mining town of Røros.

Ganz links: Winternacht im Gebirge Rondane, im Vordergrund Atnasjøen. Im Hintergrund (von rechts nach links) die Berge Storronden (2142 m), Rondeslottet (2178 m) and Høgronden (2114 m). Links: Das Dovrefjell im Mondschein. Unten links: Der Fluß Store Ula mit Rondeslottet und Storronden. Unten: Winternacht in der Bergbausiedlung von Røros.

Valdres Folkemuseum med sine 70 gamle hus ligger på Fagernes. Her kan man se hvordan man levde og arbeidet i gamle dager; spinning, baking, keramikk og folkemusikk. Neste side: Friske fossestryk i Ottaelva.

This page: Valdres Folk Museum Fagernes has 70 historic dwellings. Traditional aspects of life and work are demonstrated. Facing page: the powerful surge of a waterfall on the River Otta.

Das Valdres Volkskundemuseum mit seinen 70 historischen Wohnbauten. Hier wird gezeigt, wie in vergangenen Tagen gelebt und gearbeitet wurde. Nächste Seite: Der rießende Strom eines Wasserfalls im Fluß Otta.

Geirangerfjord, en av våre vakreste fjorder med "Prekestolen" og de berømte fossene "Brudesløret" og "De syv søstre", samt det populære turiststedet Geiranger.

These pages: Geirangerfjord, one of Norway's most beautiful fjords, dominated by "Prekestolen" and the famous "Brides' Veil" and "Seven Sisters" waterfalls. Geiranger nestles by the fjord.

Der Geirangerfjord, einer von Norwegens schönsten Fjorden, überragt von "Prekestolen" und den bekannten Wasserfällen "Brudeslöret" and "De syv Söstre". Am Fjordende – das berühmte Touristenziel Geiranger.

Øverst til venstre: Hjørungavåg med minnesmerket for slaget i 986. Øverst: Utsikt over Ytterdal ved Norddalsfjorden. Til venstre: Turistbåt i Geirangerfjord. Over: Parti fra Stranda ved Storfjorden. Neste side: øverst til venstre: Parti fra Norangsfjord, – og fra Hellesylt med fossen. Nederst fra venstre: Parti fra Volda, – og fra Ørsta.

Top left: Hjørungavåg with its memorial to the battle of 986. Top: view of Ytterdal, Norddalsfjorden. Left: a cruise ship in the Geirangerfjord. Above: view of Stranda, Storfjorden. Facing page: (top left and right) Norangsfjord, and Hellesylt, (bottom left) Volda, (bottom right) Ørsta.

Oben links: Hjørungavåg mit seinem Mahnmal zur Schlacht von 986. Oben rechts: Aussicht auf Ytterdal, Norddalsfjorden. Links: Seekreuzer auf dem Geiranger Fjord. Oben: Ausblick auf Stranda, Storfjorden. Nächste Seite, oben: Norangsfjord und Hellesylt. Unten: Volda (links), Ørsta (rechts).

91

Over: Trollveggen i Romsdalen. Oppe til høyre Romsdalshorn. Til høyre: Fra Isterdalen med Bispen, Kongen og Dronningen. Neste side: Stigfossen ved Trollstigveien med Bispen og Kongen.

Above: Trollveggen in Romsdalen. Top right: "Romsdalshorn". Right: from Isterdalen with the "Bispen", "Kongen" and "Dronningen" mountains. Facing page: Stigfossen falls, showing the Trollstigen hairpins, with "Bispen" and "Kongen" in the background.

Oben: Trollveggen in Romsdalen, oben rechts das "Romsdalshorn". Rechts: Blick von Isterdalen mit den Bergen "Bispen", "Kongen" und "Dronningen". Nächste Seite: Der Wasserfall Stigfossen, die Trollstigen-Haarnadelkurven, im Hintergrund der "Bispen" und der "Kongen".

Til venstre og nedenfor: Utsyn over Norges største fiskerihavn Ålesund. Til høyre: Molde kirke, – og fra havna i Kristiansund med "Sundbåten". Nede til høyre: Industristedet Sunndalsøra.

Facing page and below: Norway's largest fishing harbour, Ålesund. Right: Molde church. Far right: Kristiansund harbour. Bottom right: the industrial centre of Sunndalsøra.

Links und unten: Blick auf Ålesund, Norwegens größten Fischereihafen. Rechts: Die Molde-Kirche. Ganz rechts: Der Hafen von Kristiansund. Unten rechts: Das Industriezentrum Sunndalsøra.

Til venstre: Kristiansund sett fra fly. Over: Flyfoto over Molde sentrum.

Facing page: aerial view of Kristiansund. Above: an aerial view of the centre of Molde.

Links: Luftbild von Kristiansund. Oben: Luftbild vom Stadtzentrum von Molde.

Trondheim, en av Skandinavias eldste byer med bryggene ved Nidelven, Kristiansten Festning, Munkholmen og bryggene langs kanalen. Til høyre: Trondheim, byen ved Nidelven, sett fra fly.
These pages: Trondheim, one of the oldest cities in Scandinavia. Left: wharves by the River Nidelven, (below) Kristiansten Fort, (bottom left) the island of Munkholmen and (bottom right) wharves along the canal. Facing page: Trondheim from the air.
Trondheim, eine der ältesten Städte Skandinaviens. Links: Kaianlagen am Nidelven Fluß. Unten: Die Festung Kristiansten. Unten links: Die Insel Munkholmen. Unten rechts: Kaianlagen am Kanal. Rechts: Trondheim aus der Luft.

Ringve musikkhistorisk museum, Stiftsgården og Nidarosdomen er noen av Trondheims severdigheter. Neste side: Den store lysende julegrana som ved hver jul pynter byens torg.

Right: the Ringve Museum of Musical History. The Royal Palace (below) and the Nidaros Cathedral (far right and bottom right) are historic sights in Trondheim. Facing page: the Christmas fir which graces the market square each December.

Ringve Museum für Musikgeschichte. Unten: Die Königsresidenz und die Nidaros-Kathedrale sind historische Sehenswürdigkeiten in Trondheim. Rechts: Die Weihnachtstanne, die im Dezember den Marktplatz schmückt.

Fra venstre: En vinterdag i Trøndelag – og støtten av Hellig Olav på Stiklestad. Nederst: Laksesprang i fiskerike elva Namsen. Under: Fra jernbanestasjonen Hell i Nord Trøndelag. Neste side: Torghatten i Helgeland med hull gjennom fjellet.

Far left: winter in Trøndelag county. Left: statue of Saint Olav at Stiklestad. Below left: a lively salmon in the River Namsen. Below: the railway station at Hell, Nord Trøndelag. Facing page: Torghatten in Helgeland, showing the hole eroded through the mountain.

Von links: Winter in Trøndelag. Standbild von St. Olaf bei Stiklestad. Unten links: Lachs im Fluß Namsen. Unten: Die Bahnstation bei Hell, Nord-Trøndelag. Rechts: Torghatten in Helgeland, mit einem von der Natur geschaffenen Loch im Berg.

Øverst: Nordlandsbanen passerer polarsirkelstøtten på Saltfjellet. Øverst til høyre: Hurtigruta ved det gamle handels-stedet Selsøyvik i Rødøy. Rødøyløva i bakgrunnen. Over: Utsikt over øygruppen Trœna. Til høyre: Parti fra Svartisen. Neste side: Del av Svartisen, Engabreen i Holandsfjord.
Top: Nordland's railway crossing the Arctic Circle on Saltfjellet and (top right) the Express Coastal Steamer passing the former trading centre of Selsøyvik, Rødøy. Above: the islands of Trœna. Right: the Svartisen glacier. Facing page: the Svartisen glacier at Holandsfjord.
Ganz oben: Die Nordland-Bahn, die bei Saltfjellet den nördlichen Polarkreis überquert. Oben rechts: Der Express-Küstendampfer fährt am früheren Handelszentrum von Selsøyvik, Rødøy, vorbei. Oben: Die Inseln von Trœna. Rechts: Der Svartisen-Gletscher. Nächste Seite: Der Svartisen-Gletscher am Holandsfjord.

104

Forrige side: Bodø en vinternatt. Øverst: Parti ved Saltstraumen med Børvasstidan i bakgrunnen. Øverst til høyre: Parti fra Narvik med Rådhuset. Over: Midnattsol, Landegode ved Bodø. Til høyre: Korsnes i Tysfjord sett fra fly.

Facing page: Bodø on a winter's night. Top: Saltstraumen current, (top right) the town hall at Narvik, (above) the midnight sun at Landegode, Bodø, and (right) an aerial view of Korsnes in Tysfjord.

Links: Bodø in einer Winternacht. Ganz oben links: Der Gezeitenstrom Saltstraumen. Oben rechts: Rathaus von Narvik. Oben: Mitternachtssonne bei Landegode, Bodø. Rechts: Luftbild von Korsnes in Tysfjord.

Forrige side: Utsikt over Narvik med fjellheisen fra Fagernesfjellet. Denne side: Lofoten. Til venstre: Parti fra Nusfjord. Under og nederst: Henningsvær. Under til venstre: Midnattsol over Gimsøystraumen.
Facing page: panorama of Narvik from the cableway on Fagernesfjell. These pages: Lofoten. Left: Nusfjord, (below and bottom right) Henningsvær, and (bottom left) midnight sun over Gimsøystraumen.
Vorhergehende Seite: Blick auf Narvik von der Bahn am Fagernesfjell. Diese Seite: Die Lofoten. Links: Nusfjord. Unten rechts: Henningsvær. Unten links: Mitternachtssonne über Gimsøystraumen.

Forrige side: Fra torskefisket i Lofoten. Denne side øverst til venstre: Fiskevær mellom Hamnøy og Reine. Til høyre: Skomvær fyr, Røst. Til venstre: Tørrfisk på hjell. Over: Parti fra Hamnøy.

Facing page: cod fishery off Lofoten. Top left: fish landing stage near Hamnøy. Top: Skomvær lighthouse, Røst. Left: preparing stockfish. Above: Hamnøy.

Vorhergehende Seite: Kabeljau-Fang vor den Lofoten. Diese Seite, ganz oben links: Kleines Fischerdorf nahe Hamnøy. Ganz oben rechts: Skomvær-Leuchtturm, Røst. Links: Stockfisch-Zubereitung. Oben: Hamnøy.

Til venstre: "Vågekallen" 942 m ved Henningsvær i Lofoten.
Over: Utsikt over Svolvær med den karakteristiske "Gjeita" i
forgrunnen.

Facing page: "Vågekallen" 942m at Henningsvær, Lofoten.
Above: view of Svolvær with the characteristic "Goat" in the
foreground.

Links: Vågekallen (942 m) bei Henningsvær, Lofoten. Oben
Blick auf Svolvær mit der charakteristischen Gebirgsformation
Svolværgeita ("Ziege") im Vordergrund.

113

Øverst: Gammel lokalbåt ved Svolvær. Øverst til høyre: Bleik ved Andenes. Over: Hurtigruta ved Raftsundet. Til høyre: Parti fra Raftsundet med Trollfjorden til høyre. Neste side: Midnattsol ved Senja.

Top: a former coastal ship at Svolvær. Top right: Bleik at Andenes. Above: Express Coastal Steamer at Raftsundet. Right: Raftsundet with Trollfjorden to the right. Facing page: midnight sun at Senja.

Ganz oben links: Ehemaliges Küstenschiff bei Svolvær. Ganz oben rechts: Bleik bei Andenes. Oben: Kustenschnelldampfer bei Raftsundet. Rechts: Raftsundet mit Trollfjorden rechts. Nächste Seite: Mitternachtssonne bei Senja.

Til venstre: Fiske i midnattsol ved Målselvfossen, Troms. Nederst til venstre: foss i Rostadalen. Under: Parti fra havna i Tromsø. I bakgrunnen nederst Tromsdals-katedralen. Neste side: Utsikt over Tromsø med fjellheisen og Tromsøbrua.
Left: fishing under the midnight sun at Målselv falls, Troms county. Bottom left: Rostadalen falls.
Below: Tromsø harbour, with Tromsø Cathedral in the background. Facing page: panorama of Tromsø, its cableway and majestic bridge.
Links: Fischfang bei Mitternachtssonne in der Nähe des Wasserfalls Målselvfossen, Troms. Unten links: Rostadalen-Fälle. Unten: Tromsø, Hafen. Im Hintergrund die Tromsø-Kathedrale. Rechts: Panorama von Tromsø mit Seilbahn und seiner majestätischen Brücke.

Til venstre: Parti fra Lyngenfjord, Troms, med Lyngsalpene i bakgrunnen. Over: Fra Sautso i Alta, Nord-Europas største canyon.

Facing page: Lyngenfjord, Troms, framed by the Lyngen Alps.
Above: Sautso in Alta, the largest canyon in northern Europe.

Links: Lyngenfjord, Troms, eingerahmt von den Lyngen-Alpen.
Oben: Sautso in Alta, Nordeuropas größter Cañon.

Finnmark er samenes rike. De har sitt eget språk, og sine særegne drakter, og bor i telt når de driver sine reinsdyr-flokker på vidda. Til høyre: Laksefiske i Alta. Neste side: Samebryllup i Kautokeino.

These pages: Finnmark is the land of the Same (Lapps), who have their own language and dress. Herders live in tents whilst tending their reindeer flocks on the plateau. Right: a fair-sized salmon. Facing page: Lappish wedding ceremony in Kautokeino.

Finnmark ist das Land der Lappen. Sie haben ihre eigene Sprache und charakteristischen Kleidung und leben in Zelten, während sie ihre Rentiere auf den Plateaus hüten. Rechts: Ein ungewöhnlich großer Lachs. Nächste Seite: Lappen-Hochzeit in Kautokeino.

Forrige side: Turistbåt-besøk i Honningsvåg ved Nordkapp. Til venstre: Parti fra Sandfjord ved Berlevåg. Under: Utsikt mot Øksfjordjøkelen. Nederst: Midnattsol ved Hammerfest, og utsikt over verdens nordligste by, Hammerfest.
Facing page: a cruise ship in Honningsvåg, North Cape. Left: Sandfjord, near Berlevåg. Below: view of the Øksfjord-jøkelen. Bottom left: the midnight sun from Hammerfest (bottom) – the world's northernmost town.
Vorhergehende Seite: Kreuzschiff in Honningsvåg, Nordkap. Links: Der Sandfjord bei Berlevåg. Unten: Blick auf den Øksfjordjøkelen. Unten links: Mitternachtssonne bei Hammerfest, der nördlichsten Stadt der Welt.

Nordkapp (71° 10' 21"N.). Fra denne 307 meter høye, steile fjell-formasjonen og norskekystens mest kjente punkt og besøkte sted, kan man se midnattsolen fra 14. mai til 30. juli. I bakgrunnen på bildet til høyre ser man den lavere Knivskjellodden – Europa`s absolutt nordligste spiss (71° 11' 48"N.).

These pages: North Cape (71° 10' 21"N). From this 307m-high massive and most famous part of the Norwegian coast, the midnight sun can be seen from 14 May to 30 July. In the background to the right is Europe's northernmost point (Knivskjellodden, 71° 11' 48"N).

Vom 307 m hohen Nordkap-Plateau (71° 10' 21"N), dem berühmtesten Touristenziel Norwegens kann man vom 14. Mai bis zum 30. Juli die Mitternachtssonne sehen. Rechts im Hintergrund ist Europas nördlichster Punkt zu sehen, Knivskjellodden (71° 11' 48"N).

Til venstre: Kirkenes, gruvebyen som er endepunkt for hurtigruta, – Nord-Norge-bussen og landflyruten. Nedenfor: Parti fra Finnmarks største fiskevær Båtsfjord, – og midnattsol i Kjøllefjord. Neste side: Brefront i Magdalenefjord, Svalbard, – Norges utpost i Nordishavet.

Left: Kirkenes, mining town and turning point for the Express Coastal Steamer, buses and air traffic. Below left: Finnmark county's largest fishing centre – Båtsfjord, and (below) the midnight sun in Kjøllefjord. Facing page: the edge of the glacier in Magdalenefjord, Svalbard – Norway's outpost in the Arctic Ocean.

Links: Kirkenes, Bergbausiedlung und Wendepunkt für Küstenschnelldampfer, Busse und Luftverkehr. Unten: Båtsfjord, das größte Fischereizentrum von Finmark, und Mitternachtssonne am Kjøllefjord. Nächste Seite: Rand des Gletschers in Magdalenefjord, Svalbard – Norwegens Vorposten im Arktischen Ozean.